This book is dedicated to

Matron Jones
Miss Britt (our Sister Tutor)
Mrs Bunch (Practical Tutor)

And to the Class of 1 October 1956

Margaret Rulten (Rowley)
Margaret Pugh
Peggy Curtis
Phil Martin
Clarine Cave
Anthea Sellen
Diane Pyke
Maria Austen

Val Garwood
Joan Olley
Sally Lovegrove
Joyce Bourne
Deta Pink (Pinkey)
Eileen Ayres
Edna Frost
And me

HELP, I HAVE LOST MY HALO
Bedpans, bottles and broomsticks

Catherine Vaughan Thomas

SERENDIPITY

First published in 2005 by
Serendipity
Suite 530
37 Store Street
Bloomsbury
London

British Library Cataloguing-in-Publication data
A catalogue record for this book is available from the British Library
ISBN 1-84394-149-X

Printed and bound by Antony Rowe Ltd, Eastbourne

CONTENTS

1

Why Nursing?

I grew up in Wales, amongst a family of nurses on every side of the family. There they were, shining their halos and lamps, at every given opportunity. As I was a very sickly child, suffering from bronchitis, there would be no question of me joining this band of angels. Even my GP took time to tell me I would not be able to be a nurse; I was not strong enough.

Where on earth had they got the idea of me being a nurse?

I wanted to be a vet, my love was for animals. I had no idea why they all kept up about me being a nurse. No way was I going to tramp the wards, clutching a bedpan to my bosom.

I had been brought up with animals. My maternal grandfather taught me about horses and wildlife. My paternal grampa had a farm and dogs. All this will be explained in my autobiography.

I was twelve years old when I went to live with my parents in Military Married Quarters. I knew I was going to miss both my grandfathers; I still do today. Daddy was a photographer in the Royal Air Force. He had been posted to Coningsby in Lincolnshire. Now it is where the Battle of Britain Memorial Flight is housed and I have just become a Member. I hope this book will bring in some money which will go to keep my beloved Lancaster in the air.

I went to the village school, but had a few more schools before I decided what I was going to do. I was still being told I would never make a nurse, What was with everyone? Maybe they all thought if I took up nursing I would make a fool of myself.

I was quiet and happy being on my own, so in the end, having had enough pushed down my throat, as the old saying goes, if you can't beat 'em, join 'em. I went off to see the Station Medical Officer and the padre to see if they would help. The SMO gave me the address of a hospital where he had been a houseman, so I wrote to the Matron, and asked for the forms.

When I got the forms back, I answered the questions. I went back to see the SMO and padre to ask if I could have a reference. By the time I received a letter back telling me to go for an interview, I discovered Daddy had spoken to the local vet. It all came too late. I had got the bit between my teeth; now I was going to show my mother, her sister, and my grandmother what I was made of.

Mummy was on duty when I got my date for interview, so I shouted the length of the ward, yelled about the interview, and fled.

My only worry was, who was going to babysit my young brother? I had always done it.

I would show my family that I could be just as good as the rest of them. Just wait and see. In fact I became more qualified than all of them, which I will tell in my autobiography.

Now I had my interview date, the next question was, why did I want to be a nurse? I could hardly say, 'Just to show my family I am just as good as all of them,' or did I want to carry on where Florence Nightingale left off? Oh boy, what a statement; no one in their right mind would believe that I would just do the job to the best of my ability. I knew I had a hard slog ahead of me, but I was determined to be a nurse, seeing as I had been pushed into it.

One day in the future I would go back to my beloved animals. Maybe the knowledge I would gain over the next three years would come in useful.

So here I was on the train from London to my interview. That was going to change my life for a long time.

The journey seemed to take for ages. At last it entered the station. Now where? I asked the stationmaster where the hospital was; it was walking distance, so off I went past the beautiful cathedral. I would seek refuge here in the future, and also sing here.

I arrived at the hospital, still hearing the good wishes from the stationmaster ringing in my ears. The hospital was situated on the main London Road. This was going to be a busy hospital, as I would soon find out.

As I entered the front door, Reception was just there. I saw a man in uniform sitting at the desk, and I told him who I was. I was told to take a seat so I joined the other girl who was sitting there. I found out her name was Margaret and she was to become my best friend; I would name her Rowley. We still write to each other now in 2004.

We sat there like two little urchins, on two very hard chairs. It was a large hallway. There was a ward each side, and Matron's office was also situated there.

The girls looked at each other. What were they doing here? There was still a chance to run away. On second thoughts it was too late to run now.

They had just met, but little did they know they would become friends, and for the rest of their lives.

The door opposite had the word 'Matron' on it. What would she be like? What would be their reply, when she asked, 'Why do you want to be a nurse?' We could hardly reply that we wanted to be like the great lady herself, or to mop the fevered brow. Oh well, would have to wait and see.

In the meantime a lady spoke to us, telling us not to worry, Matron would not bite. It turned out she was Matron's secretary. She went in to the office, and came back quickly saying, 'You can go in now.' We both went in together. I do not know about Rowley, but my knees were knocking, and I was shaking.

Behind the desk sat a very petite lady wearing a navy blue dress with a white collar; on her head was a white frilly cap. We noticed as she got up that she had black shoes and stockings.

She introduced herself, then the questions started. She seemed to know all about us, no doubt from our references. I still cannot remember much about that interview; I suppose nerves had taken over. The interview was over, and we left the room. The secretary followed us out, but all she said was, 'See you soon.' Rowley and I had been accepted.

We made our way back to the station, and had a longed-for cup of tea. We were going to keep in touch. Rowley was going home by bus; I had to get a train to London, then another one to where Daddy was stationed.

We would not see each other now until 30 September, ready for 1 October.

2

My First Year

I arrived at the hospital the day before, still not sure if I was doing the right thing. I still had to show my family I wasn't the weakling they thought I was.

I was met by Home Sister, who would be known as 'Snugsy'. A short, rolypoly lady, she was going to be our 'Mum' for the next three years. She showed me to my room and as we entered, I had a lovely surprise: there stood Rowley. Matron thought we would like to share a room for a while. It was great to see a familiar face.

We were told to go over to the 'Sewing Room' to collect our uniforms. As we got there the ladies were waiting for us. It seemed some of our 'Set' had already been there. We collected dresses, aprons, caps, a black full length cape lined with red. Black cardigans, shoes and stockings we had to supply.

We got back to our rooms to try on our uniforms. They were fine, the only thing was that the Peter Pan white collar was going to try very hard to decapitate one's head; also the plain white belt was starched to perfection. We were also given a laundry basket for our dirty clothes.

By now it was lunch time, so we made our way to the dining room, where we would meet part of our 'Set'; the other half would be living in another part of the hospital, being brought by hospital transport each morning for school and returning at night. We were all very quiet, listening to the noise going on around us, each 'Set' sitting together. Home Sister came over to us, to tell us what to do. After we had eaten, and were ready to leave, we were going to learn Rule no 1 never go through the door before anyone senior, unless you wanted to be lynched

The rest of the day we spent looking around, until the evening meal. When t came, we waited for a couple of our 'Set' and went off to the dining room, w we were told where to sit. We had to collect our own meal; the trained staff waited on. After we had eaten, we went back to our room and got ready fo and it wasn't long before we fell asleep.

The next morning we were woken up by some prize idiot clanging a bell had told us about this part of our lives. It seemed she was practising ringing, why couldn't she go out on the cricket pitch? But no, here sh were told we would get rid of the numb feeling once we had been here but for now the noise was awful. Never mind, we would all get a cha that bell.

Having propped our eyes open with matchsticks, we saw that it w outside, like the middle of the night. We wondered if anyone wou crawled back to bed.

Getting into uniform that first morning was an effort. The white Peter Pan collar was starched to perfection; it was going to decapitate our heads before 5 p.m. Then the belt was so stiff no way could one bend down. We must make sure we did not drop anything on the floor; it would be impossible to pick anything up, one would have to remove the belt first, which in itself was a major operation. As soon as we had dressed, with just the cape to put on, all fit we made for the dining room.

As we arrived at the dining room, the noise was deafening. When we got inside we looked for anyone who looked like us. One would recognise them: they would be to afraid to move their heads. One thing we noticed was that everyone had their hair tied up with no make up and no rings, except wedding rings – there were very few of those.

As we sat down at the Juniors' table, the head and neck were being treated with great respect. Keep head still – fine, but more than a slight movement, and a notch was engraved on the neck forever. Bending down was not advisable. In the circus the magician saws someone in half, but who needed a saw to cut one in half here?

Night Sister was seated at a table trying to take Roll-call; it was like a bear garden. She was having a bit of trouble. Good thing she knew everyone.

While we were having our breakfast, we saw nurses disappearing through the door with toast and tea. We found out later that day it was for a friend who had a day off. No doubt we would be doing this sort of thing in the future ourselves.

Breakfast that day was a haze; I do not remember eating anything.

We had been told which wards we would be going to before we went into the school, where we would be going for three months. But before going to school, 't seemed the wards needed Mrs Mops, and we would be part of the cleaning team 'til 9 a.m., when we would be allowed to have a rest until 5 p.m.

vas going to male orthopaedic and opthalmology, Rowley to male medical. 'id I know about men? I only had a young brother, and a few male cousins; 'or a shock!

't to my ward, Staff Nurse was waiting for me. She showed me how to breakfast, or to finish with it.

'ents really were a bunch of looneys. When they saw me, 'Oh dear, ' baby we've got? Small, isn't she?' I was 5ft 1½ inches. Is this have to put up with? Roll on 9 a.m.

's office to get permission to leave the ward to go to school. was pleased to have me on her ward, and said I could go. 'd door for me. I told her about the teasing. How could 'ot might help. Although then they would ask what

'ods', our school. We were met by our Sister Tutor She was tall and elegant (that would please her). white collar (hers was a nice soft lacy one), and 's, finished off with the white cap (oh the cap!). 'ld be obeyed'. At least she could move her head 'tated.

She was also an ex-Army officer; no doubt she would treat us as if we were in the Army. Good thing I was brought up with the Military, so I was used to discipline.

We were allowed to choose our desks. It was funny how everyone wanted to sit in the back – no idea why! Rowley and I ended up in front. We all looked at each other, grinning like a bunch of cheshire cats, we were all so nervous.

As Sister Tutor stood in front of us, I remember her saying, 'As from now, patients come first, everything else comes second.'

What could she mean?

Another statement she made was, 'It takes three years to get your SRN [State Registered Nurse], and a few minutes to lose the lot in a Court of Law.' I had not been involved with the Law yet, so had no idea what she was talking about. We would know about that when we trained.

Then she launched into how to wear one's uniform. 'Only three hair grips in your cap, there will be no ladders in your stockings. Do not use the "ink method"; it has all been tried before. You will not 'darn' your stockings, buy a new pair [what, on our pay?]. Your hair will be kept above your collar, preferably under your cap [pity, it would have hidden the red notches on our neck].

'When you go outside the hospital, you will wear your outdoor uniform, you will not wear half uniform.' That did it; all our minds were on the same wavelength – half uniform, we would be arrested for indecent exposure. Good thing she cannot see today's nurses.

'Another thing, you must stay detached from your patients, do not get involved emotionally.'

There are fewer rules in a Monastry.

'You will not accept presents. If you are given a box of chocolates or a bottle of alcohol, it must be given to the Ward Sister to put away for Christmas, so everyone can have a share.'

Then we were told of the subjects we would be studying.

Anatomy and Physiology	
Medicine	Surgery
Gynaecology	Orthopaedics
Opthalmology	Paediatrics
Dermatology	Pharmocology
Psychology	Practical
Dietetics	Ear, nose and throat

Then there would be Theatre, Casualty and OPD Night duty

There would be Blocks to cover all these subjects, when we would learn the above, working on the wards, taking time to eat and sleep. And of course our two weeks holiday, decided by Matron. Surely, it would take ten years at least to do this lot. Someone said we had to fill all this into three years, when would we study? How were we going to survive this little lot?

Then to add to that little lot, another little surprise! Good thing we were sitting down.

'Each morning while you are in school, you will spend one hour on your wards, to help with the cleaning. Then you will be in school from 9 a.m. to 5 p.m. for your three months, after that you will be free.'

We were going to become the varicose veins of the future.

Oh yes, she nearly forgot to tell us that while we in school, we would be visiting the local water works and the sewage farm, and would be watching post mortems.

I had never done cleaning in my life. I had made my bed, cleaned my shoes, but cleaning? There we were thinking we were going to 'Slum it' in school; now we discovered we were going to be part time cleaners as well. She ended with one very important point. As from now, no Christian names would be used, surnames only; patients would be Mr, Mrs, Miss or by their title. One last piece of advice from Miss Britt: 'Remember, when you are on the wards and you are having an "off day" the patients sitting up in bed are your bread and butter. They pay your wages and without them you would not be wanted.' How true.

We already knew the wards we were going to.

Now the first thing to learn was 'Jimmy', he was our skeleton. There he stood in the altogether in front of a bunch of innocent ex-schoolgirls. Now we were going to learn what held Jimmy together. Better still, what held us together.

I knew a bit about bones from my days as a Red Cross Cadet.

Later that evening, after we had eaten, a few of us were sitting in the nurses' sittingroom, with our heads attached now to our Anatomy books. One of the nurses, senior to us, appeared, and when she saw what we were doing, she said, 'Never mind, kids, it doesn't last long, the pain gets less as time goes on.'

We decided to call it a day, and go to our beds. We fell into bed and slept until morning, when another lunatic was heard clanging the bell.

Crawling out of bed, we got ready for our breakfast. Rowley and I shared a room, but at that time of the morning (6.30 a.m.) we did not speak. We were both quiet and rather shy. When we got to the dining room, it was no different from the day before. Everyone was yelling at the top of her voice.

Night Sister was doing her Roll-call as usual. We noticed some nurses were answering twice; why? Apparently some nurses had overslept, so would get down as we left the dining room, and this was so that Sister would not know they were late. Would we be doing this as well?

When Sister said we could go, we had to wait, as we were 'small fry'. Everyone else went before us. It would have been a crime to go through the door before a senior. I got to my ward to be met by Staff Nurse again as Sister had not yet arrived. The ward was in chaos, the noise was incredible; but then, orthopaedic patients always made a lot of noise.

Already one half of the beds had been pulled out into the middle of the ward. The nurses did all the cleaning, right little bunch of Mops we were. I collected up all the breakfast dishes, took them into the ward kitchen, and washed them up ready to return to the main kitchen. I had to watch the clock. I must not be late for school, or I would be in trouble.

Before I left the ward the men had discovered I was there. I had hidden in the kitchen, but one chap yelled out, 'Look, boys there's our baby!' That did it, they all joined in. 'What a lovely baby, choochy coo,' was I sucking a dummy?

Staff Nurse and a senior nurse took me under their wings, which I appreciated; I felt like a fish out of water. The men continued to tease me. One day I might just get my own back; Before I left the ward that morning, I got, 'How long are you staying, little one?' Me they were talking about.

The beds had all been made by the night staff. The ward was always a bit untidy, as only a male orthopaedic ward can be. The majority of the patients were young men, the results of RTAs (Road Traffic Accidents), having come off their motor bikes, leaving the local firemen or ambulance people to scrape them up off the road.

The only time the ward was tidy was when the great man himself did his ward round; he was the orthopaedic surgeon, who was always rude and very arrogant.

As I was only on the ward for one hour each day, I could leave the rest of the cleaning to the nurses for now. My turn would come. If Sister was on duty I always had to ask her if I could go to school. Did she know how I felt about going to her office? Rowley always had to pass the door of my ward, so she waited for me. Some of our 'Set' who were in this part of the hospital would wait as well. As Matron's office was nearby, she must have heard us. Maybe she thought we were going to Kindergarten, not School!

When we got to school, 'She who would be obeyed' would be waiting for us, arms folded.

Today we were going to do 'Practical'. Our Sister Practical, or Mrs Bunch, was a lovely lady. She was very friendly and had a lovely smile. She was going to show us how to make beds, of which there were many.

We made any empty bed, with corners like pleats (still do it today).

Then we learnt how to make a bed with a patient in (using one of us), and how to roll a patient from side to side, without them landing on the floor. It seemed so funny, we had the giggles. The other beds were Medical, Surgical, Orthopaedic, admission beds, beds for patients coming back from Theatre, accident beds. And we all thought we knew how to make beds. We all thought it was great fun. From now on our own beds would have to be made the same as here. Home Sister would soon keep us in order.

This would all make sense once we were on our wards. The doll was used most of the time to practise on.

The famous 'corners' were used on every bed.

Once we were on the wards all this would be done as a matter of course. Do it wrong and we would be in trouble.

By 5 p.m. we were ready to go off duty. In case you are wonding if we worked all day, we were allowed one hour off for lunch. We needed that so we could all get together, to discuss if we were going to be Miss Nightingales or not. I thought not. We were all rather quiet, listening to what was going on around us in the dining room. Everyone sat at tables of seniority; no one sat with us small fry.

I could not get used to being with so many people, having been a very lonely child, and not having anyone to play with, so I found it difficult to mix now. I tried my best; that's why Rowley was so important to me. We were terrified of the Sisters, who all seemed so grand.

In the evening we would watch a bit of television, at least when it wasn't on strike, or the carpet was rolled up and we danced to a record. One record

I remember well was Frankie Vaughan's 'Green door'. When I hear it now my mind goes back to those young nurses prancing around like a herd of baby elephants.

As I have said later on, this was the night the television went on strike. We managed somehow to get hold of a screwdriver, so Rowley and I sat on the floor, took the back off, then took some 'bits' out and put them on the floor. We tried to decide what 'illness' it had. Someone came up with 'fedupitis'. We thought it had 'uselessitis', but while this was going on, Home Sister came in. She wanted to know what on earth we were doing. She really did not need us to tell her, she could see what we were doing. We were told to put it together, which we did, and with our healing hands got it going. The screwdriver was confiscated; still we always had our scissors for next time.

No doubt Matron heard about our 'second job', as TV engineers, but we heard nothing further.

The next morning there was our 'Bell Ringing Maniac'; was this what it was like in the Military?' I would have to ask Daddy when I went home.

Today we were going to learn how to take temperatures, and how to chart them. We were taking BPs (Blood Pressure) and learnt how to chart that as well; we also learnt about fluid balance charts, which included passing of urine, and IVIN (intravenous infusion) of whatever was given: normal saline, Dextrose or blood, anything the patient had drunk. It was all very important, all this was necessary as it would give an indication of any problems with the kidneys (which we had to learn about when we did our Medical lectures).

We also learnt about bottles (for men to pass urine) and bedpans to see if there was anything in them. Only we nurses had to do the charts.

Come the next day, we went over everything we had already done.

Then we came to the part where we had to learn about the 'Back Round'. Sister had laid up a trolley with a bowl, soap, talcum powder and methylated spirit; we used the patient's towel. We learnt about 'pressure areas', the back, shoulders, heels and elbows. This was done hourly, day and night, to patients who were in bed, to prevent bed sores. I was in hospital in 2003, but never had any of this done – the result was I had a sore rear end.

We used drawsheets which we could pull through to give the patient a cool spot to sit, as they could get very hot sitting continually in bed.

The night staff did their turn, as all the treatment was repeated at night.

Now we were at the time when we had to learn how to give injections. Who was going to be the guinea pig? Not me, I hate needles.

We all had an excuse, but we soon found out we were going to practise on oranges, yes oranges. Safer than letting us loose straight on a patient. We spent a good part of the day stabbing those poor innocent oranges. I bet they wished they were back on a tree in Spain.

When I had my own Wildlife Hospital, if the animals were to have injections, my thoughts went back to that bunch of nurses, learning how to do this.

Mrs Bunch had our undivided attention, but as it was 5 p.m. we were off like a bunch of rockets for our tea, and more studying.

The following week there was a film on at the local cinema. It was a hospital film called *Twice Round the Daffodils*. We decided to go and see it.

We would not have much time to change. So took off our aprons and caps, grabbed a coat, and we were off. There standing by the back door was Sister Tutor. 'Now go and change out of uniform.'

'She who must be obeyed' had spoken. We shot off to change, and were nearly late at the cinema; the film had started. As it was a hospital film we were howling with laughter. The Manager came to ask us to be quiet, but we went on laughing. He must have realized who we were, for he came down to us and gave us some chocolates. Perhaps he thought he had better humour us in case he became a patient, but it was kind of him.

While we were in school we had to do our first aid course. I had already got a couple of certificates from my days as a Red Cross Cadet, We visited the sewage works. No comment. A visit to a water works completed that lot. Invalid cookery was also on the menu, so that we knew how to cook and dish up something for the patient. We also had to make barley water, since when I cannot look at a bottle of this.

One night a few of us decided to go out. One of the gang was a pretty Jamaican girl. I went to get her, and she was in tears, so I asked what was wrong. It seemed she could not come out because we were all white, and she wasn't. Now, what to do? So I went to tell the others and we decided to help her, we managed to get hold of some flour, made a paste, and went off to Clarine's room. Gosh, she turned white in no time; the only thing was we plastered her hair; we never realized we could not get it out, and we never did go out. Our little friend had to come on duty having gone 'white'. 'She who must be obeyed' was not amused. Although it was relayed around the Sisters, no doubt Matron knew as well.

Arriving in school one morning towards the end of our time, we were told, 'Put your capes back on, we are going to the Mortuary.' The day we had been dreading had arrived. No one said, 'Do you want to go?' If we had known about this fifteen bodies would have glued themselves to their chairs.

So off we went. When we arrived there, we saw two policemen already there.

After we had watched the PM (Post Mortem), being nearest the fridge, the pathologist asked me to pass the milk.

'Where is it?'

'In the fridge.'

'Which one?'

'That one.'

I opened the door, and there along with a body was a bottle of milk.

We were now at the end of our three months, we had learnt such a lot. We took our exams and passed. Now we were being let loose on the wards, no doubt to see what damage we could do. We did find out we were favourites of our Sister Tutor. She called us her 'duffers', I ask you? We were a lovely lot, we stuck close together for our three years. We owe a lot to our tutor, but I will always remember her as 'She who would be obeyed.' Now we were going on the wards. We would have to study as well as work, tending the sick, and doing our cleaning jobs. There would always be a test or exam.

We had enjoyed our three months in school, but we were being allowed home for Christmas. I was looking forward to seeing Mummy and Daddy.

I would be able to take part in my Royal Air Force church choir. I loved singing, and had done quite a lot of singing in the past in aid of the Royal Air Force Benevolent Fund. The proceeds from this book are to go to the Battle of Britain Memorial Flight stationed at Royal Air Force Conningsby, Lincolnshire.

I had been in the first children's choir in Wales. So music was very dear to me, and still is after all these years.

The festive season was over, and here I was back at the hospital. Rowley and I still shared a room, but it would not last much longer. I was on my way to my first ward, male orthopaedic, and opthalmology (eyes). There were twenty-six beds for the 'bone' patients, and six beds for eyes.

Rowley was going to male medical. The Sister on that ward was well known for exercising her tonsils, but the Sister on my ward was short and roly-poly, and she did have a lovely smile; she did not shout.

I was going to spend three months here, or so I thought. The patients on the 'Ortho' ward were noisy, untidy males. They were mostly young men. It was not easy keeping them quiet; actually it was impossible.

Now we would all be working full time, no more ducking out after one hour. My thoughts of mopping someone's brow were soon crushed. I was led quietly out to the sluice. Silly me, I should have known where I belonged. This was going to be 'Home' for me for as long as I was here.

My job would be to clean the sluice and everything in it, plus the treatment room. Apart from taking part in the ward cleaning, I would be testing urine and sorting out dirty washing plus cleaning toilets and bathrooms. I was there to keep everything spick and span, so that everyone on the ward could come out and disrupt my domain, which I was already starting to resent.

After I had been there for a couple of weeks, Sister came out to the sluice. I was miles away, probably on a desert island somewhere. She said something to me. I was holding a large bottle of ether. I dropped it on the floor; the bunsen burner fell into the sink. I almost anaesthetized the both of us. I never did find out what she wanted, instead I had to take what was left of the bottle down to Pharmacy.

No doubt this little episode would go around the hospital, and I had only been here five minutes.

As time went by Sister always knew if someone had upset me; I could be heard banging and crashing out the sluice.

How would you feel if you spent the best of your waking time out in the sluice, then someone would come out and have the cheek to take a bedpan.

At the start of one day, I was taken into the ward, to collect dishes and wash up. Then we pulled out all the beds on one side and high dusting was done. Then we did the backs of beds, lockers, and the floor was 'bumped'. That done, it was repeated on the other side.

That finished and all the ward ship shape (some hopes) I was then banished to the ward kitchen, to wash up all the breakfast dishes, before going to the sluice to continue my cleaning job. By the time the kitchen was done, Sister was having her usual kittens, why? Matron was due to do her rounds, and as Matron's office was opposite our ward (it had to be somewhere) we were always first on the list.

The medicine round was usually complete, and any dressings would have been done, by the Staff Nurse or senior nurse. It would be a long time before I was allowed to do dressings (I thought).

For anyone who has ever worked on an orthopaedic ward, you will know it is almost impossible to keep tidy.

When Matron did appear, she sometimes took a Student Nurse with her. You had to give the patient's name, diagnosis, what they had had done, or were going to have done. If you did not know the answer, she did. There was nothing she did not know; she was great.

She knew all her staff and where they worked. I would not have to go with her yet, I thought. I had spoken too soon; it was my turn. Staff Nurse winked at me, which helped. Sister smiled to encourage me. Me! I could not believe it was happening.

Having been on the ward for a couple of weeks we were all busy with our cleaning job. I was starting to settle down, so I decided to show the men how to do high dusting (my way). I got a broom, tied a sling to the top, and set to. The men were laughing; their 'baby' was getting cheeky. While I was up to my antics, the men went quiet, and a hand went on my shoulder. I turned to see Sister Tutor standing there; she said, 'Right, nurse, now you can show the patients how it is really done. So go and get your trolley, and do it the right way.'

No one had told us that she would creep around the wards, trying to catch anyone breaking the rules. How I wished the floor would open up. I thought, that's it, she will be behind me for the rest of my training. After she had gone, I got a 'hard luck, nurse – don't worry, she was smiling behind your back'.

Another fine mess I had got myself into. No doubt another story to go around the Sisters' sitting room. Now they would all know what to expect when they had the pleasure of my company on their ward.

One thing I learned from that day, was that no matter what I was doing, or where I was, I learnt to look over my shoulder. Still do to this day.

As the morning wore on, lunch time arrived, with the trolley carrying the patients' lunch. We served it up ourselves, not like today when it comes up ready on the plate. Even on this ward there were different diets. Chips always seemed to be on the trolley, so when we took the trolley into our kitchen, with Sister in her office, the nurses finished off the chips. We should have all been overweight, but all the running about we did, we didn't have time to put on weight. If Sister had caught us finishing off the chips, she would have raised the riot act. But I bet she knew what was going on.

We learnt to drink coffee without sugar, behind the kitchen door. We were not allowed to eat or drink on duty.

The Junior always had the job of buttering the bread for the patients' tea. My thoughts were miles away. Sister came into the kitchen, and frightened the life out of me, she wanted to know what on earth I was doing. I dropped the knife, came back to earth. She wanted to know why I was buttering ants onto the bread. 'Who me, Sister?' What was she on about? When I looked down, there was an army of ants marching up the leg of the table, looking at me; they continued to march on to the bread.

Oh dear if I kept this up, the hospital would be able to write a book about my antics (what a good idea!).

I had to dispose of the bread, and start all over again, but as I said to my senior nurse, what were ants doing around at this time of year? And secondly after the teasing I was getting from that mob in there, they deserved to have ants for their tea.

The hospital being old, like any other old buildings, we had our share of wildlife: ants and cockroaches. The ward cat was no use. When I asked him why he did not chase these, he said he did not like ants or cockroaches, only mice.

Visiting time was 2 p.m. to 3 p.m. and again for an hour in the evening. Two to a bed, no children, and no one would sit on a bed, or Sister would have scalped them. Maybe that was why we did not have any infections. The Sisters of my day would stand no nonsense from anyone.

After I had been on the ward for about six weeks, the telephone out in the corridor, rang and it was for me. Someone answered it, and asked Sister if I could take it. I had a boyfriend of sorts, but his mother was ringing to tell me she did not want her son to be involved, he was going back to the girl he had gone to dancing classes with. She also objected to her son being involved with a girl who was working on a men's ward. He did not have the gumption to tell me himself, he had got Mummy to do it for him. I slammed the phone down, and, tears running down my face, hoped to get to the sluice without Sister seeing me. But there was Sister waiting for me. She guessed what had happened, so I told her. She had heard it all before. She told me what she thought of men who were tied to their mother's apron strings.

I went back in the ward, but not before Sister had told the men to leave me alone. Some hopes: I was halfway up the ward when I was hit by a flying pillow, coming my way. I caught it and hurled it back. Sister, bless her, went into her office and closed the door.

As time went on Sister was giving me more to do; instead of spending all my time in the sluice, I was doing more in the ward. She let me watch my senior nurse doing the dressings. Little did I know where all this was leading, but I would soon find out.

Then came my most embarrassing moment. In spite of the fact I had had a boyfriend, I had no idea what a male looked like without clothes on. This patient came in as an emergency, and he would be going straight to Theatre, so Sister decided now was the time to drop me in it.

'Right, nurse, follow me,' and I did, like an obedient puppy.

Arriving at the bedside,

'Draw the curtains.'

I did, then in a loud voice she said she was going to shave the patient (not his face either). I do not know who was more embarrassed, me or the poor chap, who was about my age.

'Now, nurse, I hope you have got that.' (Sniggers from some of the men.) 'You can do the next emergency.'

'Who me?'

Pity there were no trips to the Moon then; I would have been a willing volunteer.

The men never left off teasing me; now the latest was, 'Nurse, I am badly in need of a shave,' the usual idiot comments: 'Oh dear, nurse, we are growing up. Keep it up, love, and Sister can retire.' Never mind, one day I would get my own back; wait until the big white chief did his rounds.

The Orthopaedic Consultant did his rounds once a week, which was a big ordeal for us. Sister pulled the trolley with patients' notes and X-rays in. The rest of us followed on, while one of us kept the door company, in case the big white chief wanted anything.

He fired questions at us, and was very sarcastic when we could not answer.

I got away with a lot; he knew I was only a Junior and knew very little, as yet. Why was he so arrogant? On one 'Round', we had made apple-pie beds for the walking wounded, so when his Lordship arrived and asked the patient to lie down there was no way, so they sat up, knees under their chins. He was not amused, Sister said nothing. The last thing anyone expected was that we would choose the Great Man's round to get our own back.

When the Opthalmic Consultant did his visit, we only had six beds on the ward. Mr Paton was a lovely person; everyone liked him.

One day, being short staffed (as usual), nothing new, and being Theatre day, Sister decided it was time to throw me in at the deep end. I should have known someone up above was planning the next move in my young life. Sister had decided she was taking the rest of the staff to lunch, leaving me alone with this mob. I had just brought the last patient back from Theatre, and we got him into bed. I was told, 'If he asks what has been done, you will have to tell him.' I took his blood pressure etc., checked his blood drip, and was praying he would sleep until Sister came back, but the god I thought was on my side had now changed his mind. The patient looked at me and asked what had been done.

So here I was, one minute the baby of the ward, according to the men, and the next in charge of the ward and grown up enough to tell a patient what had been done. So I pulled myself up to my 5 ft 1½ inches, took a deep breath and told him he had an amputation of his leg. He was very upset, asking me how he would manage in the future, so I told him all about my childhood hero, Group Captain Douglas Bader. I had grown up knowing all about him, with Daddy being in the Royal Air Force. I had another hero, Wing Commander Guy Gibson leader of 617 squadron, the Dam Busters and his dog Nigger, a black Labrador.

I told my patient that if Gp/Cpt Bader could fly an aeroplane, swim and play golf without both legs, he would learn to walk again. (As I re-write this book, it is 2004 and I myself am learning to walk again after 2½ years; it is not easy.)

The poor man must have listened, for he told Sister I was a good little kid. I was a very junior nurse, and I did not know any better. A senior person with more experience would have given a more constructive explanation. I would learn. But I would always quote my hero.

I watched this patient do really well. He eventually went home, looking forward to his artificial leg. He also thanked me for being straight with him.

John came in with a fractured femur; he was also mentally retarded. As the ward was on the ground floor, he could watch the traffic going past, and loved to see the buses and cars.

One morning he was pointing out a bus to me. Sister heard, and came flying up the ward, and in a loud voice told me to stop wasting time, and get on with my work. I had never heard her raise her voice before. Poor John knew something was wrong, but one of the men said, 'Don't worry, we'll see to him.'

I was going to have to pick my time to teach him the different cars and buses.

John did not like cleaning time in the morning, for his bed was pulled into the middle of the ward, and he could not see out of the window. What with all the tractions and weights on the beds, it was chaos. To add to it all one morning some prize idiot threw a pillow at me, missed and hit another bed, so it was raining feathers. A cry went up, 'Staff, keep Sister in the office while we clear up.' Just our luck, Matron passed the door of our ward, but nothing was said.

It was on this ward I learnt to smoke, nothing I am proud of. I had never touched a cigarette before, but if we were behind the curtains with one of the men, he would light up, and we would have a 'puff'. Someone would ask for a bedpan, so we could have a puff. If we heard Sister coming, it was always the patient who held the cigarette. We would never have got away with this on a female ward, but the men never let us down.

While I was still on this ward one of the patients died; he was a Roman Catholic. As I was alone on the ward, I could not find a Priest, but who should came on the ward but the Rabbi. I told him what had happened, and that I could not contact the RC Padre; he said, 'No matter, I will go and say a prayer for him, and let the priest know.'

Being still very Junior, I had not really thought about what I was doing, but I did think the Rabbi was better than no one at all, and anyway I thought the Rabbi was lovely. When Sister heard what I had done, I guess she thought I was more of a lunatic than she had realized, but both the Padres stuck up for me. The RC Padre saw his patient and gave him the Last Rites. He told Sister he would never have thought to do what I had done. Saved me from Sister's gallows.

Sister was leaving me in charge quite often, inexperienced though I was, remembering I had only done three months in School, and this was my first ward. I had not long ago seen my nineteenth birthday. I should have known that something was going to happen. I was growing up very quickly, with all the responsibility I was given.

One day when I had been on the ward for about two months, it was lunch time. Sister came into the ward, and for all the ward to hear, said, 'You are to go off duty now, and come back on tonight, you are on night duty.' I was being banished to night duty. After I had picked myself up off the floor, Staff Nurse saw the look on my face, but all she said was, 'Go shine your halo, kid, I am on nights with you.'

I went off duty and made for the Nurses' Home. Home Sister was waiting for me. I was to pack up my things and move up to the night corridor, so I took everything, including my bedclothes. This corridor was only for the night time Ministering Angels. No one else was allowed there, for there was always someone asleep.

I left a note on Rowley's bed to tell her where I was. Our sharing a room was over. The corridor maid helped me make my bed, and told me to get some sleep; she would call me later. I had never slept in the day before, but I got into bed and slept.

At least I had a gentle awakening, no noisy bell being rung, just the maid coming in with a cup of tea. I could get used to this – if I was going to be looked after like this, it could be all right.

Maybe there was someone up there looking after me; only time would tell.

One thing about being on this corridor was that my view from my window was great. There in all its glory was the County of Essex cricket pitch and pavilion. One day when I was a senior nurse I would be playing out there as one of Matron's Cricket Team.

3

Night Duty

Male Orthopaedic & Opthalmology

The first job was to go around the ward with the drinks trolley: The usual Ovaltine, Horlicks, tea – but of course this crazy lot had to go a step further. 'Got any whisky, and soda, nurse?' Or 'I'll have a beer if it's cold.' I really should have given them all a glass of cold water. Usually the walking wounded did the drinks, cleared the kitchen and laid the trolley for breakfast, while we Miss Nightingales did the 'Back Round', gave bedpans and bottles. Staff Nurse did the 'Medicine Round'. This was one time when we could get our own back. We sometimes had to wake them up to take their medicines including their sleeping tablets.

Another way I could have got my own back would have been to put Senocot in their drink; only the thought of clutching bedpans to one's bosom through the night stopped us. I guess we could have put it in their morning tea, then the dear old Day Staff would be kept rushing up and down the ward, and Sister would not have been a happy bunny. Anyway we were hoping for a quiet night. (As if.)

Once the lights were out, I then had to go along to 'C' ward to help Pat out. She was a Senior nurse, about to take her finals. It was repeating everything I had done on my own ward. This was a Male Medical ward, and most of these men were confined to bed with coronary thrombosis and chest infections, along with a few diabetics, so it was a much heavier ward.

These Men were no different, though; and as soon as I got into the ward they were away: 'What a lovely baby, how long have you been here? Nurse, I need my brow mopped.'

So as Pat said, 'Take no notice, they're an ignorant lot,' but I was getting used to the men in my ward.

Very few of these men were up and about, so it was my job to clear the kitchen ready for the morning, and to empty, clean and refill the sterilizer for the morning.

I filled in fluid balance charts, very important on this ward; everything had to be perfect on this ward, or the Day Sister would have us out of bed, or she would have a screaming fit before we went to bed.

Finished here, back to my own ward, to relieve my Staff Nurse to go for her middle of the night meal. It was all quiet for a change. I put on my black cardigan and black plimsolls, having been told, 'If there is a tinkle on the telephone, ring next ward staff, take off your cardigan and put on your shoes.'

'Why?' — It meant Matron was doing a middle of the night round. In the meantime I walked around the ward, to make sure none of this mob had done a runner. Then I collapsed on a chair by the large table in the centre of the ward, keeping my fingers crossed Matron was not appearing.

After I sat down a paper aeroplane came straight for me, knocking my hat off. I got up to see who the culprit was, but not a sound was heard. I told myself I would buy a water pistol, get my own back. So I gave up and went to the sterilizing room, emptied the sterilizer, cleaned and refilled it. Then I washed all the instruments, and put them ready for me, when I turned on the sterilizer in the morning. This was all done ready to do dressings on the patients. Each ward was the same; it was always the Junior's job to do all these things. I loved it when the Ophthalmologist was coming in for our six eye patients. He had taken me under his wing, and told me all about eyes, so I would swot up anything he told me. I adored Mr Paton.

Then it would be up to me to make the 'wallpaper paste' known as porridge. I had no idea how to cook, so I was going to learn. I still have a problem in 2004 making this stuff.

When Staff Nurse came back, I had to go back to 'C' ward to relieve Pat, so I had to repeat everything. When she came back it was my turn to join the other Junior nurses in the dining room, usually to eat corned beef and tomatoes, which I now dislike, but it was great to have a break.

Then back to my own ward, where we did any 'Back Rounds' that needed doing. Then I would watch Staff Nurse writing the night report. While this was going on, there they were, an army of cockroaches, a few anyway. I got up, they fled, and so did I, on top of the ward table.

The men in this ward were full of mischief. When I did the tea in the morning, staff would be doing BPs (blood pressures) and TPRs (temperature, pulse and respiration). This lot were busy putting their thermometers in their tea, hence the reason for all their temperatures to be sky high. There was one morning when I decided to 'Chart' the high temperatures, to see what happened; when I came on duty in the evening. Sister, bless her, just said, 'I see you have been caught. Don't worry, the Registrar has got his own back. I suggested they all be given a cold blanket bath.'

Not long after I had been on Night Duty for a while, Staff Nurse showed me how to write the Report, but as I said to her, it would be ages before I had to do that. She gave me an old fashioned look, but said nothing. Neither did I, I should have guessed: someone, somewhere, was being ready to drop me in it, deciding on my future but had not yet decided to tell me; no doubt I was going to need a straitjacket very soon.

At night in the opthalmic ward the men were lying flat on their backs with their eyes bandaged, so they had no idea if it was day or night. Sometimes they were confused; very often during the night they were found standing up in their beds hanging onto their lights. They had to be checked frequently in case one fell out of bed.

By 2 a.m. one's imagination was starting to run riot; one heard noises that did not exist. With all the things going on I used to think I was going crackers, after such a short time, and me so young, and barely out of school.

I was pleased to have had the chance to work on the eye ward. When Mr Paton came in sometimes in the evening, he would tell me what he had done, and would answer all my questions. All this would come in very useful for my future, when I would work at Harley Street, and at Moorfield's Eye Hospital. The man responsible for me being interested in eyes was Mr Paton, to whom I shall be for ever grateful.

By the end of a few weeks on nights, I was getting used to sleeping during the day, and tramping the wards at night. One thing I noticed at night was the number of cockroaches who appeared if I sat down at the ward table (we had the old long wards). They would come and sit by my feet. I spoke to the Ward cat but his reply was he did not like them, he only ate mice or rats, so he would be happy for me to deal with them. He, 'no way!'

One night I had another task. Night Sister appeared and told me a patient had died; would I get ready to lay him out? I had to wait for one hour before I could start on him. In the meantime I had to get his belongings together and label them, ready for the relatives to collect.

As I was on my knees on the floor, the patient's arm must have been near the side of the bed; as I moved, his arm fell and hit me. I yelled and ended up under the bed. Poor Night Sister appeared wondering what on earth had happened. She looked at me under the bed; there I was howling my eyes out. I told Sister he had hit me. Poor old Sister must have thought she had a delinquent on her hands. She said, 'He could not have hit you, he is dead.'

But I carried on. Eventually everything was done, the rest of the ward work would have to be completed.

The 'walking' men made some tea, and gave me a cup, before Sister appeared again, with the bright idea to escort the patient down to the Mortuary. Oh well, another game to learn; it was like being at school.

After I had been on nights for a while, thinking how great life was, with no responsibilities, just being a 'Runner', my little world was about to be turned upside down. Going off one morning, to have my 'dinner' or 'breakfast', whatever, Night Sister told me to go to Matron's office before went to bed.

Now what had I done? I had not had the chance to murder anyone. My heart thumping, I made my way to see Matron. For some reason I felt lonely, and I passed 'C' ward where Rowley was working in the hope I would see her. No luck.

In Matron's office I was shot further into orbit. It seems Pat was going on leave, so 'as from tonight, I want you to go on male medical, in charge.' I could have taken to my heels and run, only I was rooted to the ground.

Male Medical

I went to bed that morning with a heavy heart. But disturbed as I was, I fell asleep and did not wake up until my cup of tea arrived. I got dressed and went to the dining room. The rest of the night staff were there, and had heard the news. They were all feeling sorry for me; all I needed was to be left alone, but they all meant well. They knew what the Day Sister was like.

I found myself creeping along to the ward. I arrived at the door, with the good wishes from the rest of the night staff ringing in my ears. I had heard all about the

Sister of this ward; if one's face did not fit, heaven help one; she stood in the corridor like a ship in full sail. I reported to her, and thought she was going to lynch me before I had done anything. After giving me the day report, in her loud Irish voice, she yelled at me, 'Just you do anything wrong.' Rowley was behind the kitchen door, waiting to wish me good luck. I was going to need more than that. So here I was on male medical in the middle of winter, what did I know? Very little. Why did Matron do this to me? The patients had coronary thrombosis, chest infections and were diabetics on insulin. (Little did I know that one day I too would be a diabetic on insulin.) I looked around the ward; where on earth do I start?

The men had heard Sister's parting shot, so they had my night schedule mapped out. At least now I would be eating first, and I would be with all the senior nurses. The men knew how junior I was because of Rowley. I got on with the ward round; the walking men did the drinks and sorted out the kitchen. I did all the charts and checked oxygen cylinders (in case I needed any!). Sister appeared to do the drug round, as I could not hold the DDA keys (Dangerous Drugs). As soon as lights were out, I was ushered into the sterilizing room, where the diabetics had got their treatment ready for the morning. They explained about their insulin. They told me I could give their injections in the morning. (The insulin I use today in 2004 is very easy although some days I ask myself – why me?)

I was going to learn fast, and would be forever grateful for their help.

My morning work done, I wasn't going to give this Sister a chance to scalp me. No matter how long I was on this ward I would try very hard not to give her the chance to do her screaming act on me. There was no cleaning to do, only the sterilizing room, plus Sister's broomstick to dust.

The day staff arrived and wanted to know how I had got on. I was still in one piece; and needed my bed. Then 'it' arrived on her daytime broomstick, parking it in the corridor. I had to give my night report. Somehow I managed to get the words out, but I was almost a wreck. That over, I was told I could go. I fled, making my way to the dining room. All the night staff were there wanting to know how I had got on. Most of them had been through all this, so they knew how I was feeling. Even Night Sister asked if everything was all right.

I dreaded every evening, and morning, when I had to face this Sister. I checked and re-checked everything. I could not have done without the help of the men. I hope if she ever reads this book, she will realize how very unhappy she made nurses like me.

How I wished Rowley had been on nights with me, I missed her company so much. This Sister liked Rowley, but disliked me, I do not know why, only that I was very Junior in charge of her ward.

The senior nurses on nights had told me: 'If you run into trouble, phone us.' Night Sister also kept her eye on me.

After she had given me the day report, she would march out of the ward; thank goodness I could relax.

As I write this book many things go through my mind. We all had an excellent training, in spite of the way we were treated.

One morning I gave the report and fled to the dining room, then took off for my bed. After 13 hours on duty, most of it alone, one needs all the sleep one can get. There I was tucked up in my bed, my black tights dripping on the radiator. I was almost in the land of nod, when I was woken by the corridor maid.

She announced, 'Nurse, Sister wants you back on the ward.'

Putting my uniform back on, including my wet black tights (Ugh) I went back to the ward, to see what I had done wrong. She was telling me to follow her into the ward; 'Now what?'

In her loud Irish voice she shrieked about a bed. 'Look at that corner, is that what you were taught in training school?'

The men had helped me make beds, and one corner was NOT the hospital corner. Silly me, I should have checked. She had got me out of bed to tell me about a stupid corner. I had to re-do it, then she said I could go.

By now I was wide awake. I took off my wet tights that were almost dry, changed and went into the town. I did not care if I got caught. At least the people outside were more civilized.

I went into the cathedral and sat down in the back, where the Padre found me howling my eyes out. He came to talk to me, and asked what was wrong? I needed someone to talk to, so I told him, I did not think I was going to carry on being a nurse; I really should have been a vet.

He listened, then told me to go back to the hospital and get some sleep.

I did.

That evening, going back on duty, I got to the ward to see the men giving me the 'thumbs up' sign. They were trying to tell me not to let her upset me. They had seen me come back, so they knew I had not had very much sleep.

When you are a young Student Nurse willing to learn and having someone finding fault and yelling for no reason, it is very disheartening. What the Medical Registrar saw in her, I do not knew. He was tall, dark and handsome. At least I had him to myself at night.

Going on that night was a real effort; I was dead beat. I was going to be very busy that night. I had a new patient, he was not very old: a rat catcher with Weil's disease.

He had been bitten by a rat, but had not gone straight to his doctor, so now he was bright yellow. He was in a cot bed in case he fell out. His liver and kidneys were affected. (I have been interested in this disease ever since and have written a paper on the subject.)

I was told by Night Sister if he moved, not to try and hold him, but to get help, so when he stood up in his bed. I stood by him, while one of the patients went to the office to pick up the phone, and drop it. The next thing I heard was footsteps. At night they sounded like a herd of elephants. They appeared in the ward while Night Sister, doctors and a porter came crashing through the door. They managed to get the patient down on his bed and sedated him. Now in 2004 I can see him hanging on to the wall, his eyes staring into space.

My patient died next day. I always tell people: 'Do not play around with rats. Stay away from streams, ponds or anywhere where the animal lives. It is not just a bite, but the urine too. If you have rats, contact your council or Rentokil.' I was very sad for that young man; he was only doing his job. So please do not throw food out in the garden, you will only attract the animal, and perhaps someone else will lose their life.

When my senior nurse (Pat) had this ward, we were blessed with a patient who was a relative of one of our Consultants. He was quiet and at the start of the evening, Pat went for her meal. Still all was very quiet, so I went off to have my meal. I had only been in the dining room for a short while when something told me to go back. I did; chaos reigned; this chap had got Pat on the bed, and was brandishing a bottle. I went up behind him, pulled myself up to all of my 5ft 1½ inches and tried to get him off, but he was 6 feet tall; he grabbed me over the bed towards him, and pushed me under the ward table.

Day Sister had been out with the Registrar. They heard the noise coming from the ward; all the lights were on, but did not come to investigate. By this time our walking patients were up and making tea. We could always rely on the men to help. By the time Sister arrived a couple of the men had hold of the chap. The public have no idea what we nurses had to put up with. Day Sister was off next day, thank goodness.

The patient was sedated, and next day was transfered to another hospital. No one can say we were bored on night duty, but it certainly made one grow up.

Another night after I had taken over the ward, one of my patients, a rather elderly little man, tried to drive me crackers. The day staff had not taken his case away from him.

So what did he do? Well, he packed and unpacked his case, so that by early morning I was crawling up the nearest wall. I thought, well only one thing to do, help him, so I got him packed and asked a patient who was awake to keep an eye on the ward, I would be a few minutes. I put my little man's dressing gown and slippers on, and took him out of the ward, up to the front desk. I told the security man he wanted to go home. 'He has his case, so please can you help him, the first taxi, bus, train or tank that passes the door, put him in it?' And I fled back to my ward. It was quiet, but some of the side lights were on, and tea had been made.

Night Sister had been called. The poor man told her, 'I think your Junior has gone batty. She left this chap here.' Sister arrived on the ward and said, 'Look what I found.' I told her what had happened. She unpacked his case and took it away from him, telling me she would sort it all out in the morning. Good old Night Sister!

Day Sister was angry that such a Junior nurse was in charge of her ward. She told Matron so, but Matron must have ignored that for there I stayed. No wonder I got yelled at so often, but I was going to show her. When I took finals, Sister Tutor found out I had credits in Medicine so I must have learnt something on her ward. I was going to have to put up with all the yelling at me, she was going to lead me a lousy life.

One night Sister came on the ward to do my drug round. After she had finished she handed me the keys. I must have looked a bit surprised, and said, 'Sister, I am not allowed to hold the keys.'

Her reply was that she would pick them up later. I attached them to my dress pocket, under my apron, hoping I would not lose them. Not long afterwards a male nurse came on the ward, and he asked me for the keys. I could not refuse, as he was a trained nurse. I gave them to him. From the ward table I could see him doing something with a syringe. I do not know what he was doing, but he locked the cupboard and gave the keys back to me. Sister came back before I went to eat, and I gave the keys back. She knew what had happened, and I was asked to say nothing. Seems he was taking morphine or heroin. I had no idea then what was going on, but I did hope I would not have to go through that again.

He left the hospital, and no doubt he would lose his licence to practise. One lesson I had learned.

I still had a couple of weeks to go before I came off nights, and was looking forward to coming off this ward, although I would miss the men. But I would not miss the lady with the broomstick! I had enjoyed my first night duty being in charge. I had learnt a lot and even grown up a little. I think.

But before I came off I had one more experience I would not forget. I was sitting at the ward table at the far end of the ward. Behind me was a balcony with six beds. By 2 a.m. my imagination would run riot. It was very quiet, then it happened; here I was, and there they were, the 'Feet'. I had heard about these from my Royal Air Force Station Medical Officer who had once been a houseman here. I had laughed at him. I thought he was joking, but no, here they were coming up the ward towards me At that precise moment one of the men came from the balcony to go to the bathroom. He was going to tell me where he was going, and put his hand on my shoulder. That was all I needed. I yelled so loud Sister heard me from the corridor outside the ward. When she came in I was in tears. My poor patient tried to tell her what had happened but all she said was, 'Oh dear, not many people see the "Feet".' Why me, was I some sort of freak? By this time the whole ward was awake; yes, you have guessed it, tea all round.

So the ward was haunted. It could only happen to me. I still had 2½ years to go, what was to become of me? Would I survive or need that straitjacket? Never a dull moment when I was around, though I was such a quiet child.

This was my last night on night duty. I was going home for my nights off, and was looking forward to seeing my parents.

First of all though, I would go and find out where I would be going when I came back.

Oh no, I was coming back here on day duty.

What had I done? Now my life would be absolute hell, her witchyness would have a field day, exercising her tonsils, and no doubt while I was away she would be polishing her broomstick.

As she was Irish I often wondered if she included me when she went to confession.

I hurried straight off duty, changed and headed for the station, I would get something to eat on the train. I was going home.

4

Day Duty

Male Medical

I came back from my rights off with a very heavy heart. I was looking forward to seeing my friend Rowley and the men I had left. I never told my parents how unhappy I was, though I did confide in our Royal Air Force chaplain. I went over to see him; I needed someone to talk to, and I knew he would not say anything. I also saw our station medical officer, who had been responsible for me going to my training school. Thinking about it, however, if I had not gone there I would not have made such a good friend in Rowley; we are still in touch in 2004. If I had told Daddy how miserable I was, I think he would have told me to give it up and go back to my idea of being a vet. If Mummy had known she would have said, 'I told you so.' So I kept quiet, I did not want the rest of the nurses in my family to know how unhappy I was. I can admit it now all the older generation have gone.

I arrived on the ward to see three of my 'set' there, so I thought, 'safety in numbers'. Sister came on duty, saw me and started off straight away. I fled to the sluice to get away from her, thinking she would leave me alone. But no, she found fault with everything I did, and I spent most of my time in tears.

The men were great; it was nothing for one of them to bring me coffee to drink, and they would grab the cup if they heard her coming. Staff Nurse began following me around, or taking me with her; it kept Sister away from me.

I became more miserable as the days went on. The men were always telling me to take no notice of her, but that was easier said than done. The longer time went on the more withdrawn I became; I also lost a lot of weight, and I could not sleep.

I vowed there and then that if I ever became a trained nurse, I would never treat my Student Nurses in this way.

Someone must have told Matron what was going on; it seems some of my 'set' were getting worried about me.

I was told Matron wanted to see me. Now what? So off I went to her office, and she told me she was moving me from the next day, I was going to female medical. Oh no, I did not get on with women too well.

So the next morning found me going through the door of a female ward. This ward was going to see if I stayed in nursing, for I had heard that this Sister was almost as bad as the one downstairs. So we should see, maybe both of them were suffering from the menopause, from what I knew about it. She could not be any worse.

Female Medical

I arrived on this ward to see a short, petite woman, Indian by birth I believe.

Someone, somewhere must have been having pity on me. The thought must have been to give me some peace. Rowley again wasn't coming with me, but three of my 'set' were already there. Two of them were from Jamaica and were good for a laugh. So hopefully things would be okay having Deta and Clarine.

This ward was a replica of the men's ward: a long ward with a balcony for six beds. The ailments were also identical, the only difference being that the women were more likely to tell Sister what was going on. We had already learnt to smoke, and on a men's ward you could have a quick puff behind the curtains; not so easy on this ward.

When we arrived on the ward, Sister realized she had a bunch of Junior nurses, and all from our 'set'. We, were known as Miss Britt's (Sister Tutor) Duffers. I've no idea why, we were a great bunch.

But Sister, having seen us, was quick to make herself known. She announced she did not expect any nonsense from us. Who, us? As if we would play her up!

This one could raise her voice, but not as bad as 'Madam Broomstick' downstairs.

This one was more sarcastic.

One day when Sister was in a bad mood, nothing new, she called us into the office. So like school children we followed each other into the office to see what she wanted. She gave us each a job to do, so we thanked her politely and went off to the sluice. We had had quite enough of being treated like idiots, so what to do? Clarine decided we should swop jobs, childish but we could not think of anything else to do. Next thing, we decided who was going to do what, and set to. When we had finished we went to look for 'Madam Sarky'. When she realized what we had done, she really let go, and had a go at us. By this time it was lunch time, so because I was off from 2 p.m. to 5 p.m., I had to stay back with her. She found me so many things to do in that hour, no doubt she would report us to Matron. But knowing how hard we all worked, we had to let off steam sometime.

I had not been on this ward long when I was told Matron wanted me. I was going back on night duty in charge of this ward. It was easy for me take over here. I did still miss the men, especially the mad crowd on my beloved orthopaedic ward, but at least I was not going to have Madam Broomstick waiting for me.

One night after we had eaten, some of us decided to go for a walk in the grounds. A couple of us were carrying toast, why? Who knows why.

As we got outside Matron's flat, one window was open. What did we do? I had been a good netball player, so the toast was handed to me, and I was told to aim it in through the window, good shot. We were like a bunch of kids. It was anyone's guess where the toast landed, no doubt we would soon find out. I often wondered why we went crazy on nights. We were always so busy that when we had free time we just took off.

No one was around to see what we had done. It was such a childish act, and not something done by senior nurses, as we were now. If senior night superintendant had seen us, she would have lynched us from the flag pole.

It seems Matron had told someone she had found two pieces of toast on the carpet, but there was no marmalade on it. We must remember that for next time. If ever.

When one of our Night Sisters mentioned it in the dining room, we looked so innocent, wonder who would do such a thing? Must have been the Juniors.

I wasn't on this ward long before I was told I was to go on the ward next door. This was female orthopaedic and surgery, and I had not worked here yet. It was almost like the men's ortho ward, except these patients had not been scraped up off the road leaving their motor bikes behind, but were mostly fractures.

Here I was, hopping from one ward to another. I was learning fast; it was about this time we were in surgical block. So we were all together, the class of 1956, and a favourite of our Sister Tutor. We were one short now, Anne Jarrold had decided to leave, so we were fifteen. Everyone wanted to sit in the back, so it was decided we would take turns. We had a reason for sitting in the back.

The doctors lecturing us thought we were a bright lot. We were not allowed to take notes, so the idea was that the back row would take the notes. Where? On the bottom of the apron. First one would start, and when the hem was full, she would nudge the next one and so on. Then we would catch up later on, so we had the lecture in writing after all. There was only one problem; when the aprons went to the laundry, well, we were in trouble. They rang Sister Tutor to complain; she tried to tell us off but could hardly keep a straight face. We had to think of something else. It was great to know the doctors thought we were bright. We could have told anyone that.

After that block I was on the move again. Now where? I had been so unhappy on the Medical wards, as both Sisters had made my life a misery. I could do nothing right; Madam Broomstick and Madam Sarcastic were impossible to work for. The nurses today would not put up with it. I really had had enough, no one had ever treated me like this before. So where was I going? To Matron for a start.

5

Tuberculosis and Thoracic Surgery

Rowley and I were sent for to see Matron. Now what had we done? The end of our first year had arrived, so perhaps it was something to do with it.

As we arrived in the office Matron smiled at us, so we relaxed.

She said, 'I want you to pack up your things and go and do your Tuberculosis and Thoracic Training. The hospital transport will collect you both at 2 p.m.'

We thanked her and left the office.

Our first year had been a hard one, but we had learned a lot. We had started with a white belt and white Peter Pan collar, to show we were the Juniors, or the 'Baby' as I was called on my first ward. Now we were senior nurses, we had a striped belt and a white 'dog collar', which was another way of severing one's head from one's neck. But we had no excuse now for not knowing the rules.

I had learnt to give injections now without the patient swinging from the light bulb.

The exam we took was in two parts. We had all passed. We had done both written and practical sections, We were pleased to get those over, so now Rowley and I would be wearing our new belts and collars. I had joined the Student Nurses' Association, so had a badge to wear on the bib of my apron.

I telephoned Mummy and Daddy to let them know the latest news, and of course to ask for money for my train fare to go home for my off duty.

Rowley and I went off to our rooms to pack, and leave notes to some of our 'set' to let them know where we had gone.

Our collars were playing up. We both felt as if we were being decapitated. Why so much starch? But we were going in uniform, wearing our outdoor coats and hat. We looked very nice. We had packed, tidied our rooms, and left the nurses' home to go to the front entrance of the hospital. We both looked at the chairs in the front hall, and were remembering how we had sat like two little urchins just over a year before, waiting for our interview. It seemed so long ago. We both had the feeling now that we were not needed here any more.

Matron's secretary saw us, and said, 'Cheer up, you two, you will have a lovely time.'

The transport arrived. We were just getting on when Matron came out to wish us good luck. We were still rather junior to be going to do this part of our training.

We arrived at our new hospital. It was all part of the group and was very large, at least to us it looked huge.

Sister who met us was the Home Sister; she was very friendly. She welcomed us and said, 'Bring your things, follow me, and I will show you your room.' We left our things and followed Home Sister down to Matron's office. She too said she was pleased to have us, and hoped we would be happy. We were told we had the rest of the day to ourselves, and we could go and look around. We thanked her, and decided it would be a good idea to report to the Sister of the ward where we would be working. She too told us she was pleased to have us. We were not used to people being nice to us, and wondered why, but decided to wait and see.

We found the dining room, so we would not starve, then we found the sitting room and found a few nurses there. We introduced ourselves, they had heard we were coming. The door flew open, and one of our 'set' appeared. We were pleased to see Val, as she said, 'Now we can have some fun.' Just as well she would not be on the same ward as us!

We arrived on the ward next morning, feeling like Juniors again. Sister was waiting for us; she seemed rather nice. We met Greta our Staff Nurse; there was one of our senior nurses as well. Jean was heading for her finals, then there was Jo, a Jamaican male nurse. Now we had to meet the patients.

There were six wards, with 66 beds on each, then we had Theatre. Our ward was male. Going along the corridor to meet the men, I thought we were going to need roller skates. There were two patients to a room, and the corridor or balcony ran along outside. If the men wanted to sleep out on the balcony, they could have their beds pulled out; they needed fresh air. How were we going to survive this lot?

The men were just as rude to me as the Orthopaedic mob had been.

Both Rowley and I looked very young. The men wanted to know what happened to me when legs were handed out. Never mind, give us time, we would think of a way to get our own back.

Most of the patients were Maltese. Now there was a start, if ever I heard something. They would go home as soon as they got the 'all clear'.

The majority of the patients were not allowed visitors by their beds. They had to talk to them from the balcony. Only those who would be going home in the near future could have relatives up to the ward. So other than that, all flowers or 'goodies' were collected and handed out to the patients.

The patients gave us a week to settle in, then they got up to their antics. Rowley and I being kept together was great, we were company for each other and were able to look out for each other. We had no idea what these men were going to get up to!

The weather was getting colder, then the snow arrived, so antics started. Grab the two girls and roll them in the snow. We were soaked, but with rosy cheeks and giggling. Sister had to send us off to change; we came back to be pelted with snowballs. Two can play at that game, so we reciprocated, but went one further, we collected a few snowballs and deposited a few in some beds.

We were busy throwing snowballs, out on the balcony, with no cardigans on, just our short-sleeved dresses, when Matron appeared and told Sister to tell those two little girls to put their cardigans on or we would be ill. No doubt Sister would have told her what had happened earlier. Poor old Sister must have wondered what she had been lumbered with.

One day, just before Matron was due to do her round, the men would not leave off. There was a laundry basket on the inside corridor by Sister's office. Rowley was standing near the basket, when two of the men grabbed hold of her and put her in it; talk about pushing a Jack-in-the Box back in its box. Matron got near, so I got near the basket and told Rowley, 'Matron near, keep quiet.'

Matron must have thought that she was as daft as us. We thought she had not seen anything and I was praying Rowley would not sneeze or cough. I held my breath. As Matron got level with me, she must have wondered where Rowley was as she knew we were inseparable. But all she said was, 'Sister, get the porters to remove the basket.' As the basket was moved, she told them to be careful with it. I bet she thought, 'Trust me to get stuck with this pair.' But it seemed we could do no wrong, lucky old us.

Another day we were grabbed and put under bedclothes. There was no end to the daft things they did.

I reckon by the time we left here we would either be a healthy pair of bunnies, or die of exposure. But I guess because we were young, we did not feel the cold.

Don't think it was all fun; it had its serious side to it. Some of the patients had lungs removed, or had been involved in bad road accidents, so there were always dressings to be done and stitches or clips to remove. There was all the resuscitation equipment to check daily. I can never remember anyone having an infection.

When we cleaned our wards daily, it was the nurses who did it all. Beds were pulled out along with lockers, and everything was washed with Lysol in water: backs of beds, window ledges, lockers, and the floor was 'bumped' using the old fashioned cleaner. The whole ward was done this way, including the treatment room, Sister's office, bathrooms and toilets, everything we did. Today in 2004 nurses are not taught these things. When a patient went home or died, the whole bed was washed, including the mattress, locker as well.

Now in 2003–4 I was in hospital as a patient, I came out from one of the hospitals with the now famous MRSA. I could not believe it, especially as I have a kidney problem.

Rowley and I had to go to Theatre one day, with one of our patients. It was going to be a major operation, taking around seven hours. We took him down and gave the anaesthetist the details of the patient; name, age, ward, blood group, what he was there for, any allergies. We had to give these details so there would not be any mistakes, and we showed the band on his wrist. We handed over notes and X-Rays. These are things I remember today.

When we got into Theatre, there was a large light over the operating table. It had mirrors on it, which meant we could see what was being done. We were sat on little stools down by the side of the anaesthetist, and were allowed to ask questions. We were also allowed to collect blood from the fridge and check it with the anaesthetist, and we were also allowed to change the blood bottles. We also checked blood pressures for him. I liked learning about anaesthetics; I found it all very interesting.

Then back on the ward. We had injections to give, of penicillin and streptomycin, which were painful for the patients. TB treatment has changed so much. After having an operation drugs such as pethidine or omnopon were given for the pain.

We were now going to work in Theatre. I must admit I was afraid of what was to lie ahead, We would be doing 'on call', but we would not be doing it together. One night it was my turn to go 'on call'. I must admit my knees were knocking. I decided to go up to Theatre to do a check. As I got to the bottom of the stairs, I could not believe my eyes. It was like Niagara Falls; water was gushing towards me. No way was I going to take the blame for this. I met one of my 'set' who asked me how I was. I said 'Wet.' Val said she was sorry; she had filled the sterilizer for me and forgotten to turn it off: result, me with wet feet.

Oh boy, were we in trouble. Sister would string us up. I got into Theatre to find one of the day nurses there. Did I know anything about the waterfall? He could see by my face I was cross, and was about to murder someone, Val came in and told Staff Nurse how sorry she was. She worked in Theatre as well. When Val was around you could bet your life something would go wrong. We had to set to and clear up Theatre, the outside landing, and down the main staircase. You could bet your life I would get called out tonight. Be just my luck.

Rowley and I found our way to the local pub near the hospital grounds. I could be called from here. When we got in the door, what did I get from doctors and male nurses alike, but: 'Who wet her pants today?' Ha ha, very funny, no doubt the patients would hear all about the water.

The anaesthetist came over and introduced himself; he was 'on call' as well. He asked what I wanted to drink – we could only have soft drinks. He had a large pint in front of him, and I asked him what it was; seems it was Coca Cola. He said, 'If you drink this, the rest of them will leave you alone, knowing you are on call; they know how long these ops take.'

I asked him what would happen if one's bladder played up. One bright spark heard my question and yelled out, 'Shout "Bucket", and someone will come running!' I know I should not have asked such a daft question. Members of my profession are never short of helpful ideas.

I said, 'Pity I am not a dog.' No answer to that; I won't tell you of other helpful suggestions that were put forward. I did like my time in Theatre, and was looking forward to working in my own hospital.

On the wards here some of the men were allowed a bottle of Guinness a day. We were given a swig out of the bottle; it was awful, tasted terrible. In spite of being so close to the men and having a swig out of their bottles, we never caught anything.

After a day in Theatre the Consultant and Registrar came to the ward, to return notes and X-Rays, and to give any further treatment they might want.

When these patients went back to Malta, there would be no further need for this size hospital. One thing is for certain: this hospital would never be the same again.

We said goodbye to Sister and the men, and went to say thank you and goodbye to Matron. She said it was a pleasure having us. We left with heavy hearts, but knowing we had another subject under our belts.

We went back to our own hospital, wondering who was going to have the pleasure of our company. We left our cases in our rooms, and went to see Matron. She had heard all about our stay at the TB Hospital. We had been given good reports.

We were eager to know where we were going to work. Rowley was going to female medical; me, I was going to 'G' ward – Men's Surgical or to give it its full name the Julian Courtauld ward. Men again – great.

6

William Julian Courtnauld Ward ('G' Ward)

I had made up my mind that if I continued to be unhappy, I would ring Daddy, and ask him to come and collect me, but I did not want to give up now, I had been happy at Broomfield. I was prepared to give this ward a chance. It was a male surgical ward, with a balcony of six beds for tonsil children.

The Sister was quite good; at least one could talk to her, and she had a sense of humour. Also there was a great Staff Nurse.

It was good having decent Staff Nurses; they were the ones who had to go to Sister's office if we wanted anything, Student Nurses did not like going in there, and we held our Sisters in awe.

The male nurse on the ward was junior to me, and good for a bit of fun. We soon became good friends. His name was John. When I left he married a girl named Anne. I had a feeling this ward was not going to be dull, but only time would tell.

This was a long ward with about twenty-two beds. The main surgery, I remember, was prostatectomies; this was where I learnt how to do 'washouts' on the men. There were other surgical ops like hernias and appendices, all sorts of things.

It was a very busy ward. After we had finished breakfast, the cleaning began. One side of the beds was pulled out, the Lyso bucket carried out, the backs of beds were washed, lockers washed, window edges, and high dusting done. I always looked over my shoulder doing this in case Sister Tutor came in. She once caught me showing the men on orthopaedics how to do this (playing around) and when she caught me, she made me show them how it was really done. Then we polished the floors, using a great bumper machine. We did so much cleaning, we could have got a job as Mrs Mops outside. The nurses did all this; we cleaned the bathrooms, toilets, sluice, and Treatment Room. We never had any infections as we have today in 2004.

Everything had to be cleaned before we did any of the dressings, or before patients went to Theatre. Sister was a very fair person, she never yelled at us. I guess she knew she would get more out of her nurses if she acted human.

John usually 'shaved' the men for Theatre. I was still very shy about doing this job which I had learnt on orthopaedics. But as we had a male nurse he did it.

When the patient was ready for Theatre, he had a label put on one wrist, with name and ward on. Whoever was taking the patient went into Sister's office to collect notes and X Rays. Sometimes the patient had a 'drip' or intravenous infusion in situ, before he went down. When you got there, you had to tell the anaesthetist the name of the patient, age, blood group, what he was down for, and the ward, then the notes and X Rays were handed over. I always liked to stay until the patient was asleep, before I went back to the ward. I got to know the anaesthetist, and he always told me what he was doing. If he was having a urinary operation done, the patient nearly always came back with a catheter in. This would drain into a bag, which hung on the side of the bed.

All this meant a fluid balance chart was kept, charting everything the man drank, or however much urine he passed. It was very important. This is where I learnt how to wash out the bladder, a very delicate thing to do. It all came in very useful in the future. Any blood or dextrose saline was recorded. The Consultant, Mr P, was great. If you showed any interest in his operation, he always had time to explain.

During the day we were busy, but it was even worse for the Night Sister and staff on the night shift. Sometimes the 'drip' was down before the day staff went off, a help for the night nurse. The night staff made the beds, because when we came on in the morning, the cleaning began.

For our 'cleaning job' we did not get paid extra; it was all part of the job. We got paid monthly £10 living in the nurses home. I was one of the lucky ones, Daddy kept me in money, paying my train fare when I went home, then he gave me money to get my black tights and all the things girls needed. Mummy also gave me cakes and biscuits to take back to share out.

It was while I was a very young Student Nurse, and had not been in the Hospital long, when Daddy was sent abroad, we had no idea where. I eventually found out he was out in Suez. That gave me something else to worry about.

Our 'set' had learnt to share clothes, so if one of us was going out with a doctor or policeman, we were dressed up, borrowing shoes, dresses, whatever, so that we looked respectable.

One day when Matron came to do her ward round she took Sister away, leaving John and me aside. We had no idea why. She went out to the sluice first, and when they came out, John and I heard her tell Sister, 'Oh Sister, the sluice is so clean one could drink tea out of those bedpans.' We heard, and had a great idea. John got the bedpan; I shot into the kitchen and made some tea. We put some in the bedpan, placed it on a tray with some biscuits, and put them in Sister's office, then we fled up the ward. Matron had left the ward, but stayed behind the wall outside the ward, waiting for Sister's reaction. She did not have long to wait; Sister came out of the office clutching her tray and hurled the lot up the ward. It was worth all the clearing up to see Matron's face. The men told Sister if they did not respect you, they would not have done that. Sister never said a word to us.

I was on this ward for April 1, and someone decided it was time to do something. I was given the job of doing the telephoning as I could imitate Matron's voice. I had to phone each Sister telling her that Matron wanted her at 10 a.m. so they all appeared outside her office. She heard them and came out to see what was going on. When they told her, she said she had not sent for them, but that she knew who was responsible. She said nothing to me. It all sounds so childish now, but we were young.

One day Sister came into the ward to me.

She said, 'I have been asked to lend you upstairs.'

'Who, me?'

'Yes, you.'

'But Sister, I am not trained.'

'Seems Matron has asked for you to go up there.'

What am I talking about? The private ward, this was the corridor above our ward and casualty, all individual rooms for private patients and an amenity ward.

One had to be an SRN to work there, so why me?

I crawled upstairs and made my way to Sister's office; a bus could have got there quicker. Sister met me and told me not to worry, 'You will be fine.' Under my breath I said to myself, 'Want a bet?'

Staff Nurse then informed me they did not normally have students on this ward, but a couple of Staff Nurses were off; that made me feel a whole lot better.

A bell rang and Staff said, 'Go on, kid, you answer it.' My knees were knocking loud enough to exchange with the church bell.

I went off to answer said bell, knocked on the door and went in. A male patient was sitting up in bed. I thought, Great, a man, and asked him what could I do for him. His reply was, 'Where did they get you? You are not a nurse.'

My blood was starting to boil, then he shouted at me, 'Shut my window,' no please, so I stood there looking at him. He again told me to close the window, so I boiled over, very rare for me, looked at him and said, 'You want your window closed, you do it,' then I fled, bumping into Sister. She saw I was upset, I told her what had happened; she told me he was a doctor, and she would talk to him.

She went in, and it seems she told him I was a second year nurse in training, on loan to the ward. He asked her to send me back in, but Sister had told him, 'She is shy, quiet and was very worried about coming to help.'

I did go back in, and he said he was sorry. I told him I was brought up not to be rude to people, then he had the cheek to say to me, 'I hear you are the baby here.' Heaven help me, I was going to murder someone before I finished training. Did I really look so young?

He did give me a box of chocolates. We were not allowed to accept presents, but I took them, and when I went back to my own ward, I shared them with the other nurses. Their response was, 'When are you going back?'

Having had my first taste of private nursing, little did I know that one day in the future I would work at Harley Street, and the London Clinic.

I did prefer my own ward for the moment, even though the men teased me whenever they got the chance.

One way we got our own back, was to apple pie a few beds, just before any Consultant did his rounds. Result – the patient could not lie down to be examined. No comment to this.

One day one of the tonsil children started to bleed. I watched how the Registrar treated it, before the child was taken back to Theatre. Many years later when I was doing private nursing, the same thing happened, and I was able to hang on until the surgeon arrived.

I was going on night duty again, now where?

I went to my 'pigeon hole' to collect a note from the previous night nurse. We always did this, then you knew what you were in for that night.

Well, panic over, I was staying on this ward, so I knew all about my patients. I went off at lunch time, went to bed until 6.30 p.m., got up, and went to the dining room to eat before I went on duty.

I arrived on the ward, and Sister gave me the report. There was one new patient for a hernia operation. I would have to get him ready next morning. He would be starved from midnight, then I would have to give him his pre med injection in the morning, which Sister would check out for me.

This ward was always busy: operations by the dozen. I reckon these men cooked up their diagnoses to keep coming in for a rest, or perhaps to get away from home for a change. But here they were; they kept me rushing around, just to make sure I had an excuse to sleep next day.

No wonder I had a slim figure — never still, no time to eat properly.

Around this time the town was having a carnival, so Sister Tutor had the bright idea of us taking part, she would call it 'Nurse Recruitment'. She hired an open backed lorry, and put a couple of desks and chairs on the back. Another Student Nurse and I had been chosen to occupy a seat there, so there was Alicia, me, Sister Tutor, perched on the back of this lorry. This was all in a good cause – promoting nursing. That was on my nights off. I still do not know why I was told to take part.

It was on this Night Duty I lost my temper for the first time.

Our Night Superintendant appeared to do a round of the ward. She never forgot me in my first year, when Rowley and a couple of our 'set', with a couple of doctors and a couple of policemen went out for the evening. We did not have a late pass, so we left our room window open (Rowley and I shared a room); the men pushed us girls in the window, and after the last girl was in, there was a great big crash. Two of the men had fallen down the coal shoot, under our window. The light in our room was out, so one of the girls yelled, 'Can someone put on the bloody light!' It went on and there sat Night Super. She reported us to Matron, and we had to report to her next morning. The doctors were there already, sporting a black eye each, I looked at them, and choked. She never told us off, but said, 'Get a late pass next time.'

So Night Super had never forgiven us. Now here I was at her mercy. I went down the ward with her, got to the new man, and my brain gave up, I could not remember what he was going to have done. That was all she needed, she yelled at me in front of all the men, told me I was useless, would never make a nurse. I snapped and shouted back, telling her if she was so clever, she could run the ward, I was going back to bed. My Junior had fled to the sluice.

I went to the office to collect my cape and bag, and stormed off up the corridor. I was fed up with being yelled at; that was not why I took up nursing.

About one hour later, sitting on my bed, feeling miserable, there was a knock on my door. I yelled out, 'What?', and in came Matron. She had got a phone call telling her I had gone off duty. I told Matron I was leaving next morning, I had had enough, Her reply was, 'Oh no you are not.' I told her what had happened, and that I would not be apologising to Sister. Matron persuaded me to go back on duty. She got a porter to walk back with me as it was late and dark. I was told Matron had followed me back, she saw Sister, but I did not do the rest of my night duty.

The whole Hospital knew what had happened, My Junior saw to that. Poor kid, she thought she was going to have to run the ward on her own.

The men told me Sister was furious, but they thought I was right to stick up for myself. Nothing very exciting happened for the rest of my night duty.

I had learnt to look after tonsil children, and was also doing bladder washouts. I was still only 19 years of age.

Now coming off nights, I was going home for my nights off. I would still not be able to tell my parents how unhappy I was. I told Padre and asked him not to say anything. He asked me to sing the anthem at the Dedication of the new church on the Royal Air Force station where Daddy was stationed; that was when Canon Giles, the Chaplain-in-Chief of the Royal Air Force, asked Padre if he could meet the little boy who had sung the anthem, Me!

The other thing I learned before I went home was that I was going to be part of Matron's cricket team.

7

Paediatrics

I came back from nights off, to be given my marching orders again, Now where? I was going to another part of our hospital, a couple of miles away. So I packed my case yet again, tidied my room, and left a note for Rowley to let her know where I had gone. The hospital transport collected me.

When I arrived at St John's, Home Sister met me and took me to my room; then I had to go and see Matron, who said she was pleased to see me. Because I had the rest of the day off, I went to meet Sister on whose ward I would be working.

She told me about one ward and I met Staff Nurse. Ruth was South African, She was great; I was looking forward to working with her.

I went off and had a look around, ready for my stay here. The ward had both male and female children up to fourteen years.

There were very young babies. I knew nothing about babies and had a lot to learn. The first thing I had to do was learn to change a napkin. At least I did know which end to put a nappy on, and where to put the safety pin. (I still have a string of safety pins from those days.)

That morning I was doing breakfasts and one toddler decided he was going to feed himself. I gave in; next thing he had put the dish on his head, and cornflakes were dripping down over each ear. Sister must have seen my face. She told me that was for starters, what else could happen? Those children who were up and about were on the floor, playing cars; they were shunting them up and down the floor and chasing each other. It was all so noisy, but the main thing was to keep then happy. It was impossible to keep the ward tidy.

I had a lot to learn about these small people. There were all sorts of things wrong with them. I had to learn about diets and making up bottles for the babies.

So here I was. Sister was going off duty, Staff Nurse had a day off, I was left in charge. Help was anybody hearing me. How do I look after this lot? There were about thirty in all. No doubt someone up there was looking down at me – I hoped so.

There were two little boys, about ten years old, who were heart cases; their prognosis was very poor. A newspaper reporter had got wind of these children and had put a piece in the paper. Somehow a copy of the paper got into the ward. The two boys saw it, and were very upset. There were photographs as well; how do you explain to any child that they might not see Christmas? If I had my way, all reporters would be banned from hospitals.

One of the visitors had brought the local rag in, and that is how the two boys saw it. I found one of them sobbing his heart out in the bathroom. We had all tried so hard to treat the boys as normal as possible. I still think about the two of them after all these years.

As you can imagine life was never dull. In fact it was the exact opposite. At that time parents did not stay at the hospital, unless the child was very ill, so we had sole charge of them all. The children never seemed to worry if their parents were not there. It also gave the parents a rest.

We learned to play with the children, and to understand all about them.

The older children were usually orthopaedic, so we got paper aeroplanes and pillows hurled at us. Now where had I seen all this before? No wonder the older version of these acted like a bunch of overgrown schoolboys. I read more comics then than I had ever read as a child.

When we were on Night Duty, it was usually quiet, though we had the 2 a.m. feeds to do. There were three nurses on at night, so there were two of us there at all times and we had the chance to clean the treatment room and fill the 'drum' with dressings and cotton wool balls, ready to go to Theatre next morning to the autoclave.

The diabetic children were a joy to watch. The seemed to know all about diabetes, testing their blood sugar, and insulin. They would quite happily give their own injections.

I loved my time with the children and learnt such a lot: children with heart problems, chests, oxygen tents, all sorts of ailments. I did hate to see them suffer. I would never have the chance to look after my own children, I never had the privilege. I have a great niece, 5 year old Emily, and her one year old brother Ben; they are great, but they are not mine,

I had come to the end of my work in Paediatrics and I was now going to do Gynaecology.

8

Gynaecology

Going from Paediatrics to Gnaecology was a big jump from children to women. I was looking forward to doing Gynae, but I am sorry to admit that women were not my favourite beings.

As everyone knows Gynae is to do with women's problems.

Again it was an old fashioned ward, one of those known as Nightingale wards: long with about thirty beds, and a couple of beds in two side wards for special cases. It was a very busy ward. We had a very nice Sister, one we could talk to.

As patients came in Sister, Staff Nurse or the houseman would explain what they were going to have done. Quite a few tears were shed here. Only now can I understand what some of the women had gone through.

One of the major operations was a hysterectomy. This meant the patient would not be able to have a family. They normally came back with an IV (Intravenous infusion) or drip. More often than not they were given blood. Today in 2004 I understand the operation is much more simple.

One patient I remember very well; she had come in very ill, and we did not think she would make it. Sister asked me if I would look after her. Mrs B. had been to a back street abortionist. She had found out she was pregnant, but had to get rid of it. I felt so sorry for her. I knew what it meant to have miscarriages, but hers was an illegal abortion. I was determined to do as much as I could for her.

It was thought she had kidney failure, as she wasn't passing urine, so I was asked to catheterise her. I did so, and I got some urine from her; I got so excited that Sister heard me and came into the side ward. When she asked what had happened, I pointed to the ceiling. There for all to see was Mrs B's urine. In my excitement at getting the urine, I had accidentally shot it from my syringe onto the ceiling. Even Mrs B laughed, bless her heart. Sister wanted to know how was I going to measure that; it could only happen to me.

The patients I could not understand were those who got pregnant and then did not want the baby, either because she was not keen, or because it wasn't the husband's. I always thought that when someone got pregnant they would be over the moon. I remember being a patient on a gynae ward; there were patients who were desperate to hold on to their pregnancies, while others were getting rid of theirs.

I know how I felt not being able to hold on to a baby. I hated to see people pushing prams.

One very good thing about this ward was the Registrar, who was Australian. I went out with him, until he went home.

One night on Night Duty, I was on with my Junior thinking we were going to have a quiet night. Just before lights out, the telephone rang. My Junior answered it and said it was for me. I should have known something was going to happen. It was Casualty; they had an emergency for me, could I get a bed ready? Why didn't I see there was a rat hidden somewhere?

My Junior said, 'They are coming,' so I told her to get the examination tray for me. I had got the bed ready. There was Staff Nurse, a Senior nurse, the casualty officer, and the patient. 'She' had a drip in her arm, sporting a blood bottle. I went to the phone to ring Bill, the Gynae Registrar, who had just gone to bed. He arrived with his day clothes over his pyjamas. Because of the crashing into the ward the rest of the patients were sitting up in bed in case they missed something.

My Junior fled, so I yelled for her to come back. Poor kid, she had never seen anything like it. After all it was now the middle of the night. The Casualty officer said he had told me to ring Bill, no doubt so he could take the blame. Good thing too for I had a funny feeling I would have been lynched Australian style.

We had got the 'patient' into bed complete with frilly nightie, then Bill decided he was going to examine the 'patient'. With that there was an almighty crash, as the 'patient' leapt out of bed, and the wig fell off to reveal one of the male nurses. The 'blood bottle' flew into the air and hit the wall; the contents went everywhere. It was of course red dye. Night Sister had just entered the ward. She of course wanted to know what on earth was going on. I let the Casualty officer have the pleasure of telling her. She must have thought she had a bunch of delinquents working for her. At that moment I was suffering from shock. My Junior was standing with her mouth open. The poor kid must have thought, is this what happens when one becomes senior? Bill was not happy; he had been got out of bed.

The Casualty mob had thought they would play a joke on me, having heard I was good for a laugh, along with having a sense of humour. At that moment my sense of humour had departed company from me. I looked at the 'blood' on the wall and floor. The two of us had to set to and clear up the mess, or Day Sister would have a fit.

The answer for anything when I trained was a cup of tea, so one of the patients did the honours, made tea all round, and cleared up the kitchen for us.

The mad crowd from casualty had gone back; I could not help wishing them a very busy night.

We two Mrs Mops set to with our scrubbing brushes, to clear up the mess. No doubt tomorrow the whole Hospital would hear about what had happened, for if the Cas staff did not spill the beans, I could just hear my patients telling Sister and their visitors. What sort of report was I going to have when I left here?

I had washed the bed and made it up ready for a real patient. My little Junior, bless her, was down on the floor scrubbing away, so I started scrubbing the wall. Would we ever get the dye off?

I often asked myself why I always got mixed up in the middle of other people's jokes. Still, one thing I could always say, I always worked hard, but always had time to join in anything that was going on.

My time was coming to an end on this ward. It would help a lot for when I did the course on Gynaecology in the future.

One thing was certain we never seemed to have any infections. Maybe this was because we were told and shown how to do the cleaning.

Bill had gone back home. I missed his company, but one day I would go to Australia. I was packing again to go back to my own hospital, and thanked Sister for having me. I went to see Matron to thank her as well. She suggested that perhaps I would like to come back when I was trained.

9

Casualty and Outpatients

When I arrived back at my own hospital, I went in search of Home Sister. I had missed dear old 'Snugsy'. She told me where my room was, so I went to unpack, Rowley appeared, it was great to see her. She told me she was in Casualty, and said, 'Guess what, you are there as well.'

I had often been sent as a Junior to help in Casualty, so it would not be too strange, also it was opposite 'G' ward. I went off to tell Sister I would be on duty the next morning. I had been looking forward to coming back here.

There were times when we went on duty at 7.30 a.m., and worked through until 6 p.m. if we were very busy. All the overtime we did, we never had it made up to us, but we never seemed to mind. Sister Stock was great to work for; she never seemed to get in a flap. The other Sister was a man, Mr Butcher, who helped me a lot.

I was taken through to Outpatients to be shown the layout, but I would be staying in Casualty for a while. The first thing I learned was how to fill in the Casualty Book. In this were all the details of the patients: name, address, age, diagnosis, and treatment. It really was a large book.

My bandaging was quite good, except that for the head. I had learnt all this as a Girl Guide and Red Cross Cadet.

So it was all going to help. We took every kind of Casualty that the ambulance men could throw at us. RTAs (Road Traffic Accidents) were in full supply. Motor bike accidents took up most of our time, speeding, coming off their bikes and being scraped up off the road, what was with them?

Then there were the walking wounded, mostly men who had got involved in pub brawls, and other fights; there were stabbings, even. Drinking and fighting have never changed over the years. Why?

One day I will never forget. Sister was off duty. The circus had come to town, one of the clowns had had an accident, Coco was brought in, and had to be plastered; there was plaster everywhere. Guess who had the pleasure of cleaning up? Right first time, talk about being plastered!

When it was very busy, it was great to watch Sister. She was so calm, would I ever be like her? Most of the time we were running about like fleas in a fit. There was supposed to be a routine, but most of the time we were too busy to think about it.

We always had the local police in; they were a very helpful lot. We got to know many of them. They were great tea makers. Another day a young woman came rushing into Casualty carrying a young child. I took the child and put it on our table, but I knew it was too late. The Casualty officer and Sister worked on the baby, while I asked her what had happened. The baby was in its pram, and she gave it a bottle which was propped on a pillow. The baby had choked. It was a tragic accident, which could have been avoided if only she had taken the time to pick the baby up and feed it. How I hate the words 'if only'.

By the weekend all the cleaning had to be done, from top to bottom.

Because of it being Casualty, the telephone was always ringing, people asking if their relative had been brought in, as he or she was missing, or had not come home. That was one call we could not answer, so we always advised them to contact the police.

One day we had a patient in with a dislocated shoulder, which had to be put back. Our Casualty officer was Hungarian. Jon was a super guy, and a good doctor; that was the day we found out he could do hypnotics. He decided to use his skills. Rowley and I were with him; she sat on the stool on the right of the patient, Jon by her side, and I was the other side of the table. The patient was asleep, and so was Rowley, she never lived that down. We all wondered if we would get a question on it for finals.

Because we were so busy we never had the chance to study on duty, so our evenings were spent in the sitting room, complete with books, usually closed. When the soap *Emergency Ward Ten* was on, we were attached to the box! Now I cannot even remember what it was about. I loved working in Casualty and never minded working overtime. When it was quiet (if ever) we did cleaning, until the next onslaught, or Rowley stayed in Casualty while I went next door to OPD (Out patients Dept). They were both part of each other and run by our two Sisters. The clinics were held from Monday to Friday, which gave us chance to clean the whole place out, although we were like a bunch of Mrs Mops during the week, in between working.

Now in OPD there were some more new things to learn. The first thing was what clinics were held on what day, and who would be taking them, Consultant or Registrar. Sister already knew two of the clinics I would want to take: opthalmology (eye) and surgery with my two favourite men. The Senior Surgeon I will never forget. When I was a Junior on Orthopaedics, he came to the ward to carve the turkey on Christmas Day. All 6 foot plus of him appeared on the ward wearing an outfit his wife had made him, none other than a tutu. I was helpless with laughing so much. The men could not believe it either; more about him when I go to work in Theatre.

The other clinics were Paediatrics, ENT (ear, nose and throat) Gynaecology, Urology, Psychiatry, Medical.

There were all the trays and trolleys to learn, how to set them up. Each doctor had his own likes and dislikes. The three clinics I liked were Medical, Surgery and Opthalmics. No one else got a look in, so Sister left me to them. I did the others when there was no one else to do them.

My time was coming to an end here. I had Theatre to do, which I was looking forward to. These three months had gone very quickly. I had loved every minute of it, all thanks to Sister Stock. Now I would be working with her sister in Theatre.

10

Theatre

At least I did not have to pack my bags, the only room I had to know about was the 'on call' room where we had to sleep when we were 'on call for Theatre', because it had a telephone, otherwise you stayed in your own room.

Like all new jobs I could feel my knees knocking; I felt like a Junior nurse again, I wondered how I was going to feel watching people being operated on, even though they would be asleep.

Watching my first post mortem had been a bit scary, but I had accepted it, and took them in my stride. I learnt a fair amount of anatomy that way.

I made my way to Theatre where the two Sisters were waiting for me. The rest of the staff had now arrived: housemen, Registrars and, being Monday, the man I did not like, the orthopaedic surgeon; to be honest I found him very rude.

Sister took me into the 'garden'; this is where the large autoclave was housed, and gloves were washed, powdered and packed ready to go in the autoclave. Great, this is where I was going to spend my time (some hopes).

The drums had been packed on the ward with dressings and cottonwool balls, to be used on the ward, but they went in our autoclave. Sister opened one drum to show me how it should be packed. There were cotton wool balls flying in all directions. She was telling me the drums would never be sterile inside, as they were packed too tightly; that was one reason we had no infections on the wards. Sister was so much on the ball when it came to packing drums.

I also had the job of seeing to equipment: cleaning instruments and packing them to go in the autoclave. The same treatment was given to caps and gowns.

I did a couple of weeks out in the 'garden', then I was encouraged to go in and watch the 'men at work'. Fine, but I fled back to my safe haven in the 'garden'.

The two Sisters decided they had to get me in Theatre, so what better than to make me the Dirty Nurse? What's that? Well, you had a board where as instruments, swabs and anything else were used they were chalked up, then it was all re-checked before the surgeon closed the operation site. That was fine.

Then it was decided I was going to 'scrub' with the surgeon. I was out in the 'garden', when the deputy Sister came flying through the door, saying, 'Come quick, we need help.' I followed her into Theatre; she showed me how to scrub and put on my gown, and I was pushed gently to the table. My favourite surgeon was operating. He told Sister to stand me on the box. Why did I have to be so short? They had all made it sound so desperate, why was everyone else holding up the wall while I was dragged by the scruff of my neck to help, help what? It was a simple hernia operation, but when my favourite man looked towards me, and said, 'You see that wasn't so bad, was it?' that was all I needed; I thought my knees would buckle.

When that was over, and I had removed my gown, I had a green top, green pants and white boots. Some bright spark said, 'Oh look, we have a gnome.'

I had gone from being the baby to the kid; now a gnome.

Now, having broken the ice, I was not worried about scrubbing up again, no stopping me now. It was only when we had finished the 'op' that I noticed most of the staff were out of Theatre, then I realised that they had all gone to all the trouble of getting me into Theatre to scrub. From now on would be fine. I would never let Sister down.

It was only because I was shy that I was slow in coming forward.

I do not know how many 'ops' I scrubbed for. Standing at the table wearing a green gown that came down towards the floor, covering my white boots, no wonder I looked like a little gnome.

The first time I was on call, everyone was hoping I would sleep all right, why? The next morning they were all there wanting to know how I was, did I sleep okay? 'Yes, why?'

It seems the room was haunted; there once was a Sister who had a boy friend with cancer; she gave him his last injection and he died. She was so upset she took an overdose of tablets, and she herself died in the 'on call' room. I was always too tired to know anything. I never worried about her, it was bad enough remembering the 'feet' on C ward.

The one thing I will never forget was the orthopaedic surgeon who I did not like; I found him rude and arrogant. One day he was doing an amputation. I was the 'Dirty Nurse' so I was watching him. He called me 'hey you'. I looked at him and he threw the leg to me. My reflex action was to throw it back. I unsterilised him, and he went mad. I fled into Sister's office and told her what had happened. She did not tell me off, but she did tell him it had taken a while to get me into Theatre, and she did not want me to refuse to go again. He asked her if I would scrub for him, but I said 'no thank you'. I had met him on my first ward, and I did not like him then.

One day we were having a discussion on premature babies, of which I knew nothing, I made a wild statement that perhaps they should be left alone. One of the housemen who was a six footer said he had been a very small prem baby, and for my efforts towards all this I was picked up and sat in the large sink of water. I could not get out, so Sister told him to lift me out, then I had to change into dry 'greens'. Serve me right for opening my mouth.

Another day one of the housemen asked me to go out with him. I told him I couldn't as I was 'on call', so he went and asked Sister if he could take me out. She was great, she told me she would stand in for me until 11 p.m., then I was to let her know when I got back, and I could finish off the rest of the night. I had just got into bed when the phone rang; we had an emergency coming to Theatre, so Keith and I met again there.

Sometimes when Mr Martin was in Theatre, he would get the idea of finishing the day's list and do some of the following day's list, so we would work all day, and into early morning. We never seemed to mind, and never complained. No wonder we learnt so much.

I do not think I will ever forget my time in Theatre, or my training as a whole, which is why I have written this book on my three years training.

11

Finals and the End of my Training

Finals were looking up, I was back on my first ward – male orthopaedic and opthalmology. It was lovely to be back on a ward where I had started the long road to my SRN (State Registered Nurse). I would have a bit more time to study. I was feeling very tired, and not very well.

The men were no better than that first mob I had nursed. Now three years later here I was back with another mob who could not let up the teasing. While I was here, we would start the written part of our finals. Mind you, the cleaning went on, including high dusting. I guess if we took an exam on cleaning, we would all pass hands down.

The written exams were over; practical now. Just before them I had earache, and felt like crawling into a corner. I did not tell anyone, although I was in a lot of pain. One day one of the patients threw a pillow at me, and it hit me on my left ear. I shrieked and landed on my knees, tears running down my face. Sister heard me, and came rushing up the ward. The guilty patient had no idea how much he had hurt me. My ear was dripping in sympathy with my eyes.

Sister telephoned Home Sister, who in turn got in touch with the ear, nose and throat surgeon. He looked at my ear and found I had olitis media. I ended up on the private wing, where I was put to bed. I got up to do my practical, it was awful.

Cotton wool had taken up residence in my ear, which was thumping like a drum. More than that, I could not hear what the examiner was telling me to do. My Sister Tutor took me out of the room, and told me I could take the practical next time. I was very upset, but was pleased to get my head on my pillow.

I decided to fly out to my parents; Daddy was stationed in Germany. When I got to the airfield I told the crew what I had, so they kept an eye on me. I needed Mummy to look after me. I had my parents to myself, as my brother was at boarding school. The station medical officer looked after me.

I stayed a month, and decided then to go home to Wales. My grandparents knew I was coming. I was going to be with my beloved grandfather; I could be his little girl again, and perhaps go on our nature walks.

I badly wanted to get back to work. I contacted one of the local hospitals, and was accepted. It was local. My cousin Wendy was a Theatre Staff Nurse at Mountain Ash. I was going to find out what nursing in Wales was like. I was at Aberdare General Hospital. The only thing was that the patients knew who I was. My four grandparents were well known.

My beloved grandfather with whom I was staying was quite sick. We discovered he had abdominal cancer. I could not bear the thought of losing him. One day he asked me if he had cancer. I said, 'No, of course not.' But I could not lie to this wonderful man who we all loved. He told me we had not been brought up to tell lies. That is my two cousins, Norma and Wendy, and me.

I made friends with a few of the nurses. Gillian used to get annoyed with me, because I was picking up my Welsh accent. She thought I was English, no way. I am Welsh and proud of it. I will be Welsh until the day I die.

Two of the other girls, Chris and Pam, and I decided to go on to do midwifery after we trained.

I had an aunt who was a midwife on maternity. It seemed a forgone conclusion I would do midder, so I was taken off men's surgical and put onto maternity to break me in, just to give me some idea of what I would have to do.

While I was there one of my aunts came in. I came on duty one morning to find an incubator plugged in in Sister's office, with a baby in it. I still have no idea what was wrong with him. Sister let me nurse him, before telling me he was my cousin; he died shortly after.

I did a short while on Children's Ward and Casualty. Then it was studying ready for finals. One Sunday I was on Casualty in charge; I was a Staff Nurse by then. But on this particular morning, all was quiet, until about 11 a.m. I had a half day and then my friend Margaret would be taking over.

A young man was brought in who had been cleaning his gun. When it went off, he had shot himself up through his chin.

Margaret was his cousin, so it would be a toss up who would be going to Chepstow with him. I said I would work the rest of the day for her to go with him. But she was not allowed to go, so I took him. All this got into the local paper. Neighbours of my grandparents came to tell them what I had done; I had not told anyone.

I had friends who had a little boy, Paul, with leukaemia. He was very ill, and his future was not good. I went to see him. He asked me if I would take him home for the weekend and could he have chips? I was going to be off, so I asked the medical staff if he could go home, and I would help out.

Paul had his weekend, and his chips. He was due back to Hospital on the Monday morning, but when his mother went to wake him, Paul had died peacefully in his sleep. He was six years old.

Pam, Chris and I were accepted to do our Part I Midwifery at Perivale Maternity Hospital, Middlesex, on 1 February 1961; we would be pupil midwives. I went on to do my Part II Midwifery at the old Paddington General Hospital in London, but that is another story.

Appendix

Dates of Interest in Nursing

1848	Foundation of Institute of Training for nurses,
1861–67	Queens District Nursing
	Jubilee QV £70,000
	Jubilee QVD £48,000
1862	First Health Visitor
1864	Geneva Convention
1869	*The Lancet* investigated OP work
1873	The National Temperance Hospital opened
1875	First industrial nurse
1896	Overseas Nursing Act
1897	Nightingale nurses' own room
1897	Outdoor nurses' uniform
1897	Paid trained nurses £10–£30 p.a.
1899	King Edward Fund for nurse training
1900	Hospitals became divided into two groups, voluntary and local authority
1905	Commonwealth nurses
1916	Royal College of Nursing
1919	Medical Officer of Health
1919	First Nurses' Registration Act (first for women)
1923	Princess Mary's Royal Air Force Nursing Service
1925	Re-named Queen's District Nurses
1928	Prison Nursing Service
1929	College gives Royal Charter
1929	Power of administration for local authority
1935	Sankey Commission – 48 regions for hospitals with pay etc.
1937	Report unknown
1938	Emergency medical service
1940	Nuffield Trust
1943	State enrolled nurses
1944	National Health Service (NHS) white paper
1945	Social services
1946	NHS commenced, to be functioning by 1948

1948	World Health Organisation (WHO) nursing representatives
1954	New nursing syllabus
1959–60	University course for nurses
1962	New syllabus
1967	King Edward Fund new limits to management courses
	Sandwich courses
	Degree courses
	Specialisation
	Clinical instruction
	Salmon report
	Platt report
1870	Education Act
1902	Balfour Act (education)
1900–9	Development of immunisation. Leeds, Liverpool etc.
1904	Formation of Works Education Association.

Adult Schools
Health and welfare
Limitation of Rose of Dr Simpson and Nun

1906	School meals, and school medical service
1907	Tuberculosis surgical hospitals
1908	Beginning of Old Age Pensioners' (OAP) Money
1910	School for Mothers at St Pancras developing to Health Visitor (HV)
1911	Insurance. Class Sister – Whipps Cross Hospital
1919	Medical health for medicine
	First State Registered Nurse (SRN)
1918	First tutors' course
1923	First state examination
1923–25	Training of Health Visitors

Research

1895	Conquest of Radium
1901	Radium – grant for pathology
1918	Drugs
1927	Insulin isolated
1905–15	Liberal government under Lloyd George

War

Implication to all research to services, use of serum and vaccine.
Position of women
National dependence on women in maintaining other work outside the home.

1924	Lady Astor – first woman MP (Member of Parliament)

History of Nursing

The Roll came into being in 1943, when the Nurses Act was passed.

At this time there were many men and women with vast nursing experience, and yet without any formal training or recognition; these people were working mainly in the geriatric field.

During the next twenty years these nurses found employment in a widening field of nursing in hospitals, public health and in industry.

In 1964 a new syllabus of training came into force to meet the ever increasing need of the bedside nurse. A two year training was stipulated together with specifications as to the theory and practical knowledge required before the training school could submit the nurse for the state assessment set by the GNC (General Nursing Council).

On successful passing the examination the nurse would complete the remaining months of training and then become a state enrolled nurse (SEN).

There are other trainings open to the SEN in many fields of nursing, in hospital, on the district, in industry and in the field of public health.

In this history we must begin by examining the medical notions current among ancient peoples. From their crude conceptions of the healing art have originated all modern methods of caring for the sick, both those that we call medical or surgical and those that we class as nursing.

Egypt

The first place must be given to Egypt, because in its dry sands were preserved the papyri containing our most complete examples of ancient medical literature. Like other peoples of antiquity the Egyptians regarded disease as due to causes partly natural, partly supernatural. In Egypt as in India, China and primitive Greece, medicine was held to be of divine origin. A famous physician, *IMHOTEP*, who lived about 3500 BC, came by degrees to be regarded as a god, and in later days was identified by the Greeks with their god of healing, *ASKLEPIOS*. The name *IMHOTEP* means 'he who cometh in peace'.

Medicine branched off from magic and began its independent career early in Egyptian history, for already in the Pyramid Age there are records of man bearing the title physican as distinct from that of magician. One remedy was proved millions of times: for preventing the hair (lashes) from pricking the eye, Frankincense I, Lizards Blood I, Bats Blood I, dip the hair until the eye is well.

The Egyptians even had their own specialists: a different doctor for different parts of the body. e.g. Cyrus King of Persia (d.529 BC), had the most skilful of all the Egyptian eye doctors.

Babylonia and Assyria

If a man's head is full of scabies and itch thou shalt take sulphur. Mix it in cedar oil and anoint him.

China

Reputed to have used anaesthetics as long as AD 190.

India

In the first place a mansion must be constructed, spacious and roomy. One portion at least should be open to the currents of the wind; it should not be exposed to smoke, or the sun, or dust, or injurious sound or touch or form of scent ... after this should be secured a body of attendants of good behaviour, distinguished for purity or cleanliness of habits, attached to the person for whose service they are engaged, possessed of cleverness and skill, endowed with kindness, skilled in every kind of service that a patient may require.

Endowed with general cleverness, competent to cook food and curries, clever in bathing or washing a patient, well conversant in rubbing or pressing the limbs, or raising the patient or assisting in walking or moving about, well skilled in making or cleaning beds, competent to pound drugs or in waiting upon one that is ailing, and never unwilling to do any act that they may be commanded (by the physician or patient) to do. This is as far back as AD 200.

Deaconesses and Early Christian Hospitals

Sick visiting was mentioned in the Bible in the parable of the Good Samaritan. Matt. 25: 'I was sick and ye visited me.' The first woman mentioned as a Deaconess was Phoebe. Deaconesses in the early church constituted a recognised order.

'For there are houses where thou [i.e. the Bishop] canst not send the Deacon unto women because of the heathen, but thou shalt send the Deaconess.' We can assume that the Deaconess's life was one of devotion to the sick and needy for hospitals were unknown in those days and nursing would probably occupy a considerable share of the Deaconess's time.

Monastic Hospitals

In the Benedictine rule (about AD 480) it is expressly stated that the care of the sick must be given attention before and above all else that they may be ministered unto, as though indeed it were unto Christ.

There existed large twin communities of men and women both being usually under the control of an abbess. That the house of the two sexes were kept rigidly apart is shown by the following extract.

If one of the monks fall ill, either in his own or in a distant monastery, he must not lie in the monastery of nuns, lest his body grow well and his soul sick. All sick monks must lie in a monastery of men, uninvited by any relations, by strangers or by maids. If however it should happen that a woman is sent by the Abbess with broth for the sick man, she may, in the presence of a male servant, give to him, but not venture to stay with him.

Hospitals in Constantinople

'You may see them walking along, sometimes blind, sometimes lame, sometimes having some other illness. I myself have seen an old woman waited on by a young one, and a blind man led by a seeing person, and a footless man using the feet not of himself but of others, and a handless man led by the hands of other men, and children nursed by strange mothers, and paralytics served by able-bodied mortals. So the number of those who were supported was double, some being served, and some servers. Thus Alexius gave attendants to each incapcitated man.' Anna is speaking not of trained attendants, but of inmates who waited upon one another, as was the case in English Infirmaries before their reform.

The Secular Orders (not Monastic)

The so-called 'secular orders', a term used to distinguish them both from the Knightly orders and from regular communities with perpetual vows, became very active in the early thirteen century.

All secular orders were not devoted to nursing, but among those which made it their main work one of the most important was that of the Holy Ghost founded towards the end of the twelfth century in Montpellier by Guy de Montpellier.

There were Brothers and Sisters of this order which has always been associated with nursing in large hospitals.

The Knights Hospitallers of St John of Jerusalem
The Teutonic Knights, The Lazarists

The first military nursing orders, founded by some Italian merchants of Amalfi, founded two hostels, one for men and one for women. The men's was dedicated to St John the almoner, and that for the women, dedicated to St Mary Magdalene.

It is generally assumed that from these two hospitals originated the subsequently famous order of the Knights Hospitallers of St John and Jerusalem, though this connection has been disputed and it has been thought that Peter Gerrard was its creator.

Besides their original houses in Jerusalem and at Margat, the knights wherever they established themselves built a hospital, and those in Rhodes and Malta can still be seen today, no longer hospitals but museums and government buildings.

There were also apparently women members of the order who had some nursing duties. They were not allowed full membership, but were called lay sisters.

They took vows of poverty, chastity and obedience and lived outside the Monastic precincts. The rule said women were to be admitted because services to cattle and to the sick persons in hospital were better performed by the female sex!

Also at this time were the Teutonic knights founded by a German and also that of the knights of St Laxerus (taken from the Lazerus of the parable in Luke 16 who was regarded as a leper) and at the beginning of their order, the Grand Master had to be a leper, but this was stopped in 1253 because of the shortage of lepers.

The Regular Orders

Among the regular nursing orders the one about which we know most is that of the Augustinian Sisters of the Hotel Dieu of Paris, one of the oldest purely nursing orders of nuns. The Sisters' round of incessant work, only broken by religious offices and but two meals a day, seems to our modern eyes unnecessarily hard, and their number inadequate to deal with all the patients, since in common with other hospitals the practice was here followed by putting up to six patients in a bed. Their daily routine was as follows.

They rose at 5a.m., and went to chapel while the senior made her tour of duty. All then dispersed at six to their respective work and those in the wards put out the lights and attended to the patients.

They served them their two daily meals, going to their own meals in relays, spending the afternoon in doing what could not be done in the morning and at seven retired to their dormitory, while the watchers were in charge of the wards and the senior Sister did a late tour of duty by the light of a torch. In addition to the ward work they had to do the hospital washing in the Seine. This was divided into the great wash (every six weeks) for which six Sisters and three novices were required and the little wash done every day which employed three Sisters.

Domestic Nursing

It was the custom to include in the education of girls of the upper class some knowledge of medicine and a smattering of surgery, more especially of that branch concerned with the treatment of wounds. This knowledge was regarded as a matter of course. The country housewife was expected to look after the bodies of the household in sickness as well as in health and it was necessary for her to have a skill in physics and surgery.

> The knight is brought in wounded and then
> She and her maids, those ladies three.
> Of all my gear they spoil me.
> Both of my hauberk and mine actown [quilted jerkin]
> Washed me and laid me down
> With her own hands, while as the milk
> She stopped my wounds full of silk

And then laid me into bed
That was with silken sheets spread.

(Old English language)

The treatment of a feverish patient is described further:

He is covered up, hot bricks are put to warm the bed, his feet are rubbed with vinegar and salt, his head is bathed with rose water and after he has started to sweat more covers are put on and he is given a posset of milk of almonds.

From the Reformation and Renaissance to the end of the eighteenth century

After the Dissolution (1535–7) of the Monastries by Henry VIII and the consequent collapse of the monastic system, including hospitals, great misery prevailed among the poor since England alone among European countries possessed no hospital system.

In 1347 the City of London petitioned Henry VIII's son Edward VI for leave to take over the largest Hospitals, St Bartholomews (Bart's) St Thomas's (Tommy's) Bridewell and Bethlehem, their reason being the lack of accommodation for the sick. This marks the beginning in England of the civilian control of hospitals and hence lay nursing was begun.

In one respect the older monastic custom was advantageously copied, and that was in re-training a woman head or Matron over the nurses, and in keeping for the person in charge of a ward the title 'Sister'. Moving further into the century probably the highest level of nursing was reached in the household of the Gentry where the Mistress felt herself to be responsible for the training of her children and servants in every branch of the domestic arts amongst which were reckoned both medicine and surgery. Extract from the diary of Lady Hoby (about 1600).

After I prayed then I dined, then I walked and did see a sick man.
I went to a wife in travail of child about whom I was very busy.
After my private prayer I dressed my patients and then dined after I walked abroad ... dressed my patient and so returned to private prayer and meditation.
On the Lord's Day after the sermon, I dressed other poor folks. I dressed the hand of one of our servant boys that was badly cut.
Dressed a poor boy's leg that was hurt. This day Blackeborn cut his foot with a hatchett. Next day dressed the Blackeborn's foot.

No Doctor was as a rule available in the Country, and the whole district depended upon the lady of the Manor's Ministrations.

The standard of care, never very good, became particularly bad at any time of unusual stress or emergency, such as an epidemic and the nurses (so called) in the great plague of London in 1665 are described as dirty, ugly, unwholesome hags. In 1730 an English physician, Thomas Fuller, gives a very early description of a nurse.

Of a Nurse: Thomas Fuller

It is desirable that she be

1. Of a middle age, fit and able to go through the necessary fatigue of her undertaking.
2. Healthy, especially free from vapours and cough.
3. A good watcher, that can hold setting up the whole course of the sickness.
4. Quick hearing and always ready at the first call.
5. Quiet and still, so as to talk low, and but little, and tread softly.
6. Of good sight, to observe the sick, their colour, manner and growth and all alterations that may happen.
7. Handy to do everything, the best way, without blundering and noise.
8. Nimble and quick, coming and doing everything.
9. Cleanly, to make all she dresseth acceptable.
10. Well-tempered, to humour and please the sick as much as she can.
11. Cheerful and pleasant, to make the best of everything, without being at any time cross, melancholy or faint hearted.
12. Constantly careful, and diligent by night or day.
13. Sober and temperate, not given to gluttony, drink, or smoking.
14. Observant to follow the Physician's orders duly, and not to be so conceited of her own skill as to give her own medicines privately.
15. To have no children.

A tribute paid by the English Captain Knox to the excellence of the French nuns nursing after the Battle of Quebec (1759) clearly implies that to him this was a surprising novelty.

> When our poor fellows were ill, and ordered to be removed from their own odious regimental hospitals to this general receptacle, they were indeed rendered inexpressibly happy, each patient had his own bed with curtains allotted to him and a nurse to attend him.

> Every officer has an apartment to himself, and is attended by one of these religious Sisters, who, in general are young, handsome, and fair, courteous, very reserved and very respectful.

The 18th Century in England

There were a lot of Hospitals being built.

The Westminster	1719
Guy's Hospital	1725
St George's Hyde Park	1728
The London	1740
The Middlesex	1745
Liverpool (RVI)	1749
Manchester Royal Infirmary	1753

At St George's Hospital a man and his wife were engaged at salaries of £8–10 per annum to be Messenger and Matron respectively.

Sometimes the qualifications of a nurse chosen were merely that she had been a patient. She began as night watcher and was then admitted as nurse. The first nurse was addressed 'as Squire', she is not even honoured with Mrs or Miss.

19th Century Nursing

This was of course the era of the Crimean war and Florence Nightingale and I think most of you know that she was the beginning of nursing as we know it today.

Another great woman was Elizabeth Fry (1780–1845) famous for her work among prisoners. In 1840 she started in London a small society of nurses to work among the poor. She wished to call them Protestant Sisters of Charity, but in deference to criticism changed the title to the Institute of Nursing Sisters (which today might be akin to the Queen's District Nursing Services).

Another powerful champion of nursing reform, though neither a doctor nor a nurse, was the novelist Charles Dickens (1812–70). His forcible pen attacked, among many other abuses, the degraded condition of the nurses of his time. In *Martin Chuzzlewit* (first published in 1844) his immortal portraits of Mrs Sarey Gamp and her scarcely less famous colleague Mrs Betty Prig depict far more vividly the depths to which the ordinary professional nurse had sunk.

Florence Nightingale

Born 12 May 1820
Died 13 August 1910

Florence because she was born in the city of Florence, Italy.

Foundations of knowledge from the immense amount of travel with her parents.
Created a good relationship with a Mr and Mrs Sidney Herbert.

Studied in Paris in 1853 with the Sisters of Charity. In 1854 Sidney Herbert was Secretary of War. To have women nurses in the army was immodest, unthinkable, revolutionary. Thus Florence Nightingale went to the Crimea and at Scutari there were 1,715 sick and wounded. Four miles of beds and only eighteen inches apart.

Commenced Nightingale Training School for nursing at St Thomas's. 15 Probationers were admitted for a year's training on 9 July 1860 (over a century ago). Supported by money collected from the general public; some of the probationers had to pay to be taught nursing and this carried on until the late 1930s.

Florence died in her sleep in 1910 and is now buried at East Willow in Hampshire besides her parents and not in Westminster Abbey.

All that is written on the gravestone is F.N.

The Battle for Registration

The establishment of a Register for practising nurses would have made it possible to remove the name of any nurse who had discredited her profession. But the militant qualified nurses demanded more from registration than this; they wanted to draw a firm line between those who were fitted to practise as nurses and those who were not.

But how was a qualified nurse to be defined? Training alone was not held to be sufficient test. The training hospitals were issuing certificates but the quality of the training given varied widely. Thus some central body was to be set up which would decide which hospitals were providing adequate training and which were not. In addition, there was to be a national examination to ascertain whether each individual trainee had benefited sufficiently from her course; only those who had passed this examination were to be admitted to the register.

The first move to form a professional association (The British Nurses Association) with these objectives in mind came from the lady pupils. The leader was Miss Ethel Gordon Mansion. She came from a prosperous and influential family. Her father was a doctor and her stepfather was an MP. She entered the children's hospital in Nottingham as a paying probationer in 1878 at the age of 21.

After one year she went on to the Manchester Royal Infirmary. From there she was appointed Sister of Charlotte Ward at the London Hospital, where she was always complimented on the apple-pie order of her cupboards and on the freshness of the lovely flowers in her care.

Early in 1881 three years after starting training in a children's hospital she was appointed Matron of St Bart's hospital at the age of 24. One evening she had read that St Bart's Hospital in the city of London required a Matron.

Here was her chance. She decided she would become that Matron.

Early next morning she dressed with the utmost care and laid a little emphasis on her great age (24) and armed with particulars of her experience and glowing testimonials, she presented herself at the astonished Secretary's office at 9 a.m. punctually and revealing the reason for her visit. After promising to help her in her ambition, he made the necessary inquiries and a week later she was summoned to the Board meeting and informed that her application had been successful.

In 1887 she married Dr Bedford-Fenwick who played an active part in medical politics and she retired from nursing to devote her energies for the next sixty years to the organisation of the profession. Mrs Bedford-Fenwick had a very forceful personality. She pressed her views persistently and without compromise throughout her long career in nursing politics. She demanded the highest possible standard of nursing and she believed that this could be secured by confirming entry to the profession to the daughters of the higher social classes.

She thought that firm educational and financial barriers should be erected in training schools to keep out undesirable recruits. Steps should be taken to protect them from criminal nurses as at present there was not any sort of discipline or control over these women. 'They go to prison, they come out again, and they go on nursing.' Registration would improve the character of the women who went in for nursing. There was also a desire for parity with the medical profession and greater prestige in the types of hospital managements: a committee of businessmen, Mrs Fenwick stated, will often select a woman with housekeeping experience rather than one who has qualifications which make her the best head of a nurse training school. In their way it is often of more importance that she should know the price of mutton.

Of course not everyone shared Mrs Fenwick's view on registration – in particular Miss Nightingale firmly opposed it. She felt it would do great damage to the cause of nursing. Seeking a nurse from a Register was very much like seeking a wife from a Register as is done in some countries.

Her principle objection was that registration would involve the introduction of examinations for nurses. The professional competence of a nurse could not be judged in this way. All an examination could test was knowledge and a nurse could acquire all the knowledge she needed in six months.

If a public examination were to keep place of assessment by the individual hospital, she feared that less attention would be given to personal qualities in the selection of some nurses.

The most vigorous opposition to registration came from the two hospitals in which Mrs Fenwick had nursed, from Sidney Holland of the London and from Dr Moore of St. Bart's. They were firmly opposed to any measure which would narrow the field of recruitment to the nursing profession. Sidney Holland did not sympathise with the nurses' claim for professional status. 'We want to stop nurses thinking themselves anything more than they are, namely, the faithful carriers out of the doctor's orders. Some nurses consider that they ought to have fourteen footmen to wait upon them.'

The argument about the registration of nurses was not just a battle of principle; there were also vested interests and personal feuds. Some provincial hospitals' Matrons favoured registration as they thought that this would place the certificates they issued on a parity with those of the smart London hospitals, their own status would thus be enhanced and more of the best type of girls might come to them for training instead of going to the London hospitals.

There may in addition have been a few Matrons who were opposed to registration, seeing it as a challenge to their own position. They may have feared the interference of an external authority which would attempt to control the training they were providing.

Thus in 1887 the Hospitals Association at the request of Miss Wood (Superintendant of the Gt Ormond St Children's Hospital) held a meeting at Burdetts House in Porchester Square, started the *Nursing Mirror* and the hospital publications and the foundation of King Edward's Hospital Fund for London – and of course Mrs Bedford-Fenwick was at the meeting which became very stormy.

After the meeting in 1887 each group proceeded with its own plan. The hospital association under the leadership of Burdett established a Register of trained nurses and issued a badge.

The Register was open to those who proved they had worked for at least one year on the staff of a hospital or infirmary and had been trained in the duties of a nurse. A testimonial of good character and entrance fee of 2/6 (two shillings and sixpence) and a payment of one shilling a year thereafter were also requested. But little use of this was made of the Register either by hospitals or by nurses.

Meanwhile the British Nurses Association agitated for an official register of nurses. In 1889 a mass meeting was held in the Mansion House and in the same year Dr Fenwick proposed and got the General Medical Council of the BMA (British Medical Association) to pass the resolution in the following terms: that an Act of Parliament should as soon as possible be passed for providing for the registration of nurses.

To have a better asset the BNA approached Princess Christian (daughter of Queen Victoria) who consented to be their Patron, so they had Royal patronage. Registration could be achieved in two ways. First there would be an Act of Parliament. To prevent this, Miss Nightingale got her friend Mr Rathbone to prepare a very confidential brief for the Duke of Westminster and organised a memorandum signed by influential nurses. Because of unrest in the RBNA (because before the Royal charter Mrs Bedford-Fenwick was a permanent President of the Association) and because of the Royal charter it was suggested that all members had to be re-elected and Mrs Bedford-Fenwick lost her permanent Presidency. After this both she and Dr Fenwick retired from the association, but for the next years tried to do it a lot of harm.

The climax came in 1896 when the association passed a resolution opposing state registration – was Miss Nightingale behind this move?

The suggestion by the doctors was that the nurses might do them out of a job and of course the money. Whatever the cause, Mrs Bedford-Fenwick and her allies temporarily lost control of the RBNA. She had however other irons in the fire, and in a later year she started the Matrons' Council of Great Britain and Ireland for all those Matrons who wanted State Registration.

In 1902 the Society for the SRN was settled. In 1904 the two bodies came together to form the National Council of Nurses.

Of course the list organised by the Association had never really caught on in the way Mrs Fenwick had hoped it would.

A more important precedent for the nurses was the Midwives Act of 1902 which introduced a Register for Midwives. The First Bill went into Parliament on this subject in 1878 and by 1891 both the GMC (General Medical Council) and RCP (Royal College of Physicians) supported registration – this was because of the great toll of maternal and infant deaths from unqualified midwives.

Each year from 1904 to 1914 a Registration Bill was laid before Parliament.

Those who favoured Registration were reminded that there were forces who were opposed to it, and those who opposed it were reminded of the many who had favoured the Registration and so on.

In 1914, 457 Matrons opposed Registration and yet 500 were in favour – the total exceeded the number of Matrons in Great Britain.

1914–18 Recruitment was up because of War.

1915 276 Territorial Nurses had gone abroad. Owing to the war more ladies arrived for nursing – the Recruitment increased from 35 to 150 in a month.

1916 – Military Hospitals, one trained nurse per bed. In Voluntary Hospitals it was one trained nurse per 19 beds. In Poor Law Institutions – one per 44 beds. In Voluntary Hospitals under Private Management 1 nurse per 4 beds.

VADS (Voluntary Aid Detachments) originated in 1909. St John and Red Cross at the end of war had 1,20,000 Members.

1916 – Royal College of Nursing began in March for the purpose of admitting nurses to its register. The College recognised for training civilian hospitals and infirmaries with at least 250 beds. There had to be a Resident Medical Officer and at least one course of lectures a year and an examination for Qualification. Male nurses and mental nurses were excluded from the Roll.

Still a battle raged over the BNA and RCN Registration, If women were to have the vote, then the demands of some hundred thousand electors belonging to the nursing profession could not be ignored. The House of Lords even seemed in awe of the opposite sex – after some heated arguments Registration was accepted in principle, but all was not so as the RCN and RBN wanted to take sides so that the battle went on. Eventually the Minister gave up and brought in its own Bill – by December 1919 the Minister's Bill had received the Royal Assent.

The Register consisted of the following parts

   a. A general part containing the names of all the nurses who satisfied the conditions of admission to that part of the Register.
   b. A Supplementary part – male nurses.
   c. A Supplementary part – fever nurses.
   d. A Supplementary part – children's.
   e. Any other described part.

There is no fever or children's part in the Register. Persons without formal training admitted at the onset – providing they could prove they had done nursing for the past three years – fee 1 guinea. Total 40,451; expected 80,000.

In 1925 the First State examination was held and 4,000 nurses were admitted to the Register by the examination.

Portals of entry – age 17½ years.

Education.

The number of failures were large – hence the commencement of the Education Test for probationers in 1937. The Union at the, beginning of the century, was 'The National Asylum Workers Union'.

May 1930	Staff Nurses £62 per Annum.
	Sisters £80 per Annum.
	Hours of work 60 hours per week, to 80 hours.
1919	RCN suggested 52½ per week, to 84 hours
	Night Duty.
	After the war 48 hours per week.
1930	Probationers' life:
	Petty restrictions, petty tyrannies and plenty of heavy domestic work.
	In by 10 p.m. (one late pass per week).
	Routine domestic work. 8 hours a day.
	Strong discipline in the wards.
	Night Duty – forbidden to sit by the fire or wear or shawl. Slowly as time passed conditions improved and are still improving.
1943	EEN Mrs Bedford-Fenwick still going strong, opposed it.

1948   Whittley Council comprising 64 Members.
            Staff – 41.
            Management – 23.
            Fights all our battles, rewages, hours etc.
            World Health,
1851   12 nation conference in Paris, requarantine, regulations, abortive
            attempts.
1874   Vienna Conference.
1888   International Council for women.
1889   London. International Council of Nurses presided over by
            Mrs Bedford-Fenwick, an English Matron,
1918   League of Nations.
1949   San Francisco conference of nations, epidemics. International
            Quarantine,
1953   Code of Ethics for nurses.

Care and Storage of Drugs

1. Laws are laid down by Parliament for care and storage of drugs.
    These are known as STATUTORY REGULATIONS.
2. Local rules are also made at Hospital and group level, known as Local
    Rulings.
3. *The Pharmacy and Poisons Act 1933.*
    a. Registration of Sellers.
    b. Registration of Qualified Pharmacist.
    c. Statutory poisons laid down by Home Office.
    d. Poisons list for (1) and (2).
        (1) To be sold by Registered Pharmacist only.
        (2) To be sold by Registered domestic seller of ammonia.
4. The Poisons Rules 1952. (Amended 1965).
    17 Schedules of which only 2 are relevant to Nursing.

a. *Schedule I*
   (1) Stored in locked cupboard.
   (2) Adequately labelled.
   (3) Ordered by MC.

   Schedule 4A
   (1) Prescription

   Name and address of doctor and patient.
   Name of drug.
   Quantity of drugs to be supplied.
   Dosage (if prescription to be repeated)
   Signature of doctor and date.

Dangerous Drugs Act 1965

Dangerous Drugs Regulations 1965
This is concerned with the Control of Narcotics.
There are 5 parts to the Act but only one section is relevant to Nursing.

Dangerous Drugs Act for Hospitals

1. Prescriptions must be signed by Registered Doctor.
2. Stock ordered from Pharmacy in special book. (836 pad) signed by Ward Sisters or Deputy.
3. Drugs delivered in sealed container. Receipt signed by Ward Sister.
4. D.D. stored in locked cupboard, within a locked cupboard.
5. Only Dangerous Drugs in this cupboard.
6. Records kept in ink.
7. Waste accounted for.
8. DDA Books kept for two years.
9. All D.D.S.I.

b. *Provisions for Storage and Administration*
Exemption for substances containing small amounts of narcotics too small for danger.

5. *The Therapeutic Substance Act 1956.*
Controls manufacture, purity, potency for certain drugs, also sale, supply and dispensing of same.

    a. Vaccines
    b. Ligatures
    c. Insulin
    d. Antibiotics
    e. Curare
    f. Blood
    g. Heparin etc.
    h. Dimercafrol and derivatives
    i. Cortecosteroids and trophin